Taking the Waters

Early Spas in New Zealand

Ian Rockel

Government Printing Office  Publishing

Wellington, New Zealand — 1986

Cover photograph: The Rotorua Bathhouse c. 1909.
Rotorua Museum.

ISBN 0-477-01369-4

Typeset in 11/12 Palatino by Wordset Enterprises Limited,
Wellington.
Printed and bound by Wright and Carman, Upper Hutt.

Contents

Acknowledgments

I owe thanks particularly to the staff of the National Archives, who went out of their way to help with this project. Special thanks are also owing to the staff of the Auckland Institute and Museum Library and to the staff of the photographic section of the Alexander Turnbull Library.

I acknowledge the following sources of material used in this book: Department of Tourism and Publicity; Department of Health; Rotorua District Council; Alexander Turnbull Library; National Museum; National Archives; Auckland Institute and Museum; Auckland Public Library; Whakatane Museum; Canterbury Museum; Canterbury Public Library; Hocken Library; Opal Hot Springs Ltd, Matamata; Miranda Hot Springs Oasis; Awakeri Hot Springs; Hartley Consolidated Ltd, Waiwera; Snoline Spa Hotel, Maruia; Waingaro Thermal Baths; Te Aroha and District Museum; Taupo Regional Museum and Art Centre.

I thank the following people who kindly supplied me with information: the Cleaver family, Matamata; Mrs Pilling, Waingaro; Mrs Kidd, Miranda; Mrs Wilton, Maruia Springs; Mr G. Timbs, Awakeri; John Dustin, Te Puia Springs Hotel; Annabelle White, Department of Lands and Survey, Tongariro National Park; Bruce Collier, Whangarei; Ken Niven, Taupo; Molly Elliott, Devonport. I thank also my father, Mr S. Rockel of Rothesay Bay, Auckland, for assistance with research.

Lastly, I would like to thank my wife Jean, who typed the manuscript and put up with difficult moments.

Author

Born in Blenheim in 1939, Ian Rockel was educated in Puketapu and Hastings before attending Wellington Teachers Training College from 1957 to 1959. Teaching, the completion of a BA degree and other work in New Zealand and England followed, until he trained as a librarian in Wellington, thereafter working at the Alexander Turnbull Library and the National Museum. From 1967 to 1969, while supply teaching in London, Ian Rockel enjoyed completing as much as possible (for someone not working in a British museum or gallery) of the Art Galleries and Museums Association Diploma.

From 1970 until 1986 he was Curator, then Director, of the Rotorua Museum, a job which gave him an interest in photographic history and led to his writing *Taking the Waters*. He has contributed to a book on the history of Rotorua and was an editor of a Rotorua District Council publication commemorating the Tarawera eruption. An established poet, who has read his own work in Wellington and Auckland, Ian Rockel is now a full-time writer; he has many novels planned. He and his wife Jean live in Rotorua with their 3 children and many cats.

1 The Great Spa of the South Seas

For the sophisticated European of the nineteenth century, a spa was much more than just a health resort. The famous spas of France, Germany and Britain were elegant social and cultural centres. Most who took the cure did not do so primarily for medical reasons, but to see and be seen by high society. If you were in residence at Bad Hofburg while the Prince of Wales shed several pounds, you were someone of significance.

The spas' cultural tradition, too, was long and impressive. Dostoevsky wrote *The Gambler* after his experience of the Baden-Baden casino, and Berlioz composed the opera *Béatrice et Bénédict* for the opening of the opera house there. Turgenev described life at Baden-Baden in his novel *Smoke* and Brahms wrote his Second Symphony while easing his coffee-stricken liver at the famous German spa. Franz Lehar composed the most popular of all light operas, *The Merry Widow*, at Bad Ischl, where the various Strausses penned waltzes between seasons. Goethe met Beethoven at Karlsbad and Dvŏràk conducted there.

English caricaturists Thomas Rowlandson and George Cruikshank found a variety of subjects at Bath and Cheltenham. The German spa, Nauheim, famous for its treatment of heart disease, provided the setting for Ford Madox Ford's superb novel *The Good Soldier*, in which an American woman has just enough strength to carry on an elaborate adultery. Edith Wharton portrayed New York society at Saratoga Springs. Long before, Jane Austen wrote of the genteel and the pretentious at Bath; Tobias Smollett of the scrofulous and randy. Tuscany's Bagni di Lucca was a favourite haunt of Shelley, Byron and Heine. Lamartine's *Le Lac* was written after an episode at the spa of Aix-les-Bains.

Such great spas had a long history, often stretching back to Roman times. Bath, for instance, was originally known as Aquae Sulis, Baden-Baden as Aquae Aureliae, Aix-les-Bains as Aquae Allobrogum.

By the late nineteenth century, realising the potential of New Zealand's mineral waters, particularly at Rotorua, the Government was keen to create a spa in the South Seas which would compete with the great resorts of Europe. Many parts of New Zealand were suitable for such development and promotion, if bathhouses, pumps for drinking water, accommodation and good access could be provided.

But how could New Zealand hope to compete with the richness of European spa culture and tradition? When the first bathhouses were built here, New Zealand's total population was only 500 000, and even when the new Department of Tourism and Health Resorts took over the development of the Dominion's spas in 1901, the population was a mere 815 000.

FRANZENSBAD.

THE FIRST MUD BATH IN THE WORLD.

Possesses the strongest Chalybeate Springs and Digestive Ferruginous Alkaline, Glauber's Salt, and Lithia Waters.

Four large Bath Establishments with Natural Carbonic Acid, Chalybeate, Mineral, Brine, and Stream Baths ; Thera-peutic Mud Baths ; Steam and Hot Air Baths and Electric Light and Tub Baths. **Medico-Mechanical Institute. Inhalatorium.**

Cure for Anæmia, Chlororis (Green Sickness), Scrofula, Rheumatism, Gout, Catarrh of the Respiratory, Urinary and Digestive Organs, Habitual Constipation, Nervous Diseases, Neurasthenia, Hysteria, Women's Diseases, Wasting Diseases, Cardiac Diseases (Weakness, Inflammation, Neurosis, and Fatty Degeneration of the Heart).

The Best known Baths in Austria for Heart Diseases.

SEASON—May 1 to September 30.

PROSPECTUS FREE.

The powerful Lithia Water of the " Nataliequelle," the Ferruginous Water of the " Hercules " and " Stephanie " Springs, and the Mineral Acid Water of the " Francis " Spring, and of the Salt and Meadow Springs, **the medicinal properties of which are well known,** are forwarded to all parts of the world.

For information respecting the Cure, address the MAYOR.

An advertisement in *Murray's Handbook for Travellers in New Zealand*, 1893, giving travellers the alternative of a European spa. Franzensbad was one of a great many spas in the Austro-Hungarian Empire. Note the suggestion in the advertisement that neurosis is a disease of the heart. *Rotorua Museum.*

New Zealand may not have wished to emulate the affectations of a stratified European society, but it was this society, with its wealth, that was needed to fund and develop a great South Seas spa. Such a clientele would, moreover, expect sophistication and ornamentation, not hot mud and pumice, tussock and manuka, and the most basic of amenities. Such amenities were very much the rule during the first 20 years of development under the Lands and Survey Department; at least one of New Zealand's spas had no one living in the vicinity at the time Government works began.

The difficulties New Zealand faced in trying to compete with the northern spas were exacerbated by the fact that the European resorts had a background of royal patronage. Buxton, in Derbyshire, for example, became famous after Mary Queen of Scots used the water there to relieve her rheumatism. Much later, at Bad Ischl, the Emperor of Austria-Hungary managed to shoot 50 000 animals while his empire crumbled around him.

2

JAMES MUIR, ✳ ℋydropathic Specialist,

LATE OF MOFFAT & CRIEFF, SCOTLAND;

MATLOCK, BUXTON, AND HARROGATE, ENGLAND;
AND ROTORUA.

BY APPOINTMENT TO TE AROHA HOT SPRINGS DOMAIN BOARD.

ADVICE given FREE to Ladies and Gentlemen on the judicious use of the Baths and Drinking Waters.

Hydropathic Treatment and "SMEDLEY" System of PACKING administered in connection with the Baths.

TERMS BY ARRANGEMENT—PAYABLE IN ADVANCE.

HOURS OF CONSULTATION, in Domain Board Room: 9 to 10.30 a.m., 5 to 5.30 p.m.
.   .   Daily (Sundays excepted).   .   .

Private Residence: c o NURSE BATES,
Convalescent Home, Te Aroha.

This Scottish expert in hydropathic techniques practised at Te Aroha in the 1890s. The forgotten spa of Moffat, where Muir formerly treated patients, was visited by Carlyle, Hume, "Ossian", Boswell and Burns. *National Archives.*

For Rotorua and Te Aroha, New Zealand's 2 main nineteenth-century spas, it was a tall order to try and provide a dignified architecture that could challenge the Royal Crescent at Bath, the Pittville Villas at Cheltenham or the Trinkhalle at Baden-Baden. And how could brass bands, "a distressful piccolo"[1] or "a lame piano"[2] attract visitors from a country where Mrs Siddons, Garrick and Edmund Kean had performed at Bath or Tunbridge Wells, and Handel, Haydn and Liszt had played at Bath?

Although New Zealand had had little practice in providing European ostentation and elaborate ritual, the colony did have an advantage in terms of natural resources. As the first Medical Officer at Rotorua commented: "The hot springs of New Zealand vary in composition and strength from those strong enough to dissolve a galvanised iron bucket to the mildest saline diuretic which can be imbibed at the rate of one gallon per diem with impunity."[3] Only the seriously ill, however, may have been interested in the fact that New Zealand's distant geothermal waters could offer a much greater range of temperatures and minerals.

As a country with a very small population, New Zealand was dependent upon the return from wealthy overseas visitors to make expensive improvements. If New Zealand were a Mediterranean island, Rotorua, Te Aroha and Hanmer would undoubtedly be spas of international importance. But 19 000 km was just

3

In about 1900 German Apollinaris table water is being advertised at Ohinemutu in front of the 1872 Tama-Te-Kapua house. No doubt the intention was to suggest that Apollinaris was drunk throughout the world, even among the thermal waters of Rotorua. *Rotorua Museum.*

too far to travel to experience Antipodean waters. Without the income from rich European and American tourists, New Zealand Governments eventually turned away from financially unrewarding spa development to more politically worthwhile projects. As long, too, as New Zealand rejected the idea of either casinos or a special tax, 2 factors which helped to provide the amenities of the great spas, elegant Europeans would continue to reject the rawness of colonial bathing conditions.

Many small New Zealand towns of the 1880s and 1890s had little more to show a visitor than dusty streets, weatherboard buildings and corrugated iron chimneys. There were 2 attempts to provide spa facilities which would attract overseas travellers — the ornamentation of Te Aroha's Cadman Baths in 1898 and of the Rotorua Bathhouse in 1908 — but the wealthy still failed to come in large enough numbers. They might journey out to see the Pink and White Terraces, the Wanganui River, the Southern Alps and lakes and, at the end of the century, the southern fiords, but they could take the cure much more comfortably at Aachen (Aix-la-Chapelle), Harrogate or hundreds of other spas far closer to home.

Another area in which New Zealand could not hope to compete was that of medical supervision. At the European spas every moment of the cure was supervised, but until the arrival of the Government Balneologist in 1902, taking the cure in New Zealand was a largely empirical exercise, with people bathing as and where they liked. Before 1902, medical personnel were often involved in urgent cases that had nothing to do with balneology (the science of bathing). They could not possibly oversee people's bathing arrangements with the same thoroughness as a large specialist staff.

Although the New Zealand Government's dream of creating the great spa of the South Seas was never fully realised, many thousands of New Zealanders and tourists have, for more than a century, enjoyed the healing and relaxing waters of a variety of spas and springs. It is these that are the subject of this book.

References

1   *The Dominion*, 12 January 1911.
2   *Rotorua Chronicle*, 6 January 1914.
3   Lewis, T. Hope. "The Thermal Spas of New Zealand" in *Cook's New Zealand Guide*, 5th ed., 1905.

2   Too Few People and Too Far Away

The attempt to create spas, either for New Zealanders or for overseas visitors, began in the first half of the nineteenth century, with Robert Graham's purchase of Waiwera, and the Colonial Surgeon's comments about Tikitere, near Rotorua. Dr Johnson wrote in 1847: "when the true character of its waters as remedial agents has been ascertained . . . it will be a part of the country much resorted to by invalids."[1] Sir George Grey promised, in 1848, that a sanatorium would be built at Tikitere but the idea was not developed. (Had there been no challenge to Ngati Rangiteaorere's ownership of land in the area, Rotorua town may have developed at the east end of the lake, in the area between Te Ngae, at the junction of the Tauranga and Whakatane Roads, and Tikitere. Because of the disagreement between the owners and a neighbouring tribe the Government's interest in Tikitere lapsed.)

The main advocate of developing geothermal resources for medicinal purposes was the former Premier of the country, the Hon. William Fox. In 1874 he wrote to the Premier, Julius Vogel, "to draw the attention of the Government to the great value of the sanitary provision which nature has made in the districts described [the Volcanic Plateau]. I think the time has come when something practical might be done to utilise that provision." It may, he added, "prove a source of great wealth to the colony".[2]

It is significant that, between Fox's letter and 1880, nothing was done to develop the mineral and geothermal waters (apart from Graham's private development at Waiwera). New Zealand's first period of widespread spa development coincided with William Rolleston's term of office as Minister of Lands, from October 1879 to August 1884. Unfortunately, because many of the department's files were burnt, we cannot estimate Rolleston's personal interest in the hot water resources of the country. During those years, however, Rotorua, Te Aroha and Hanmer began their existences as spas.

It was at this stage that the original Thermal Springs Districts Act was passed, in 1881, whereby only the Government could purchase hot springs areas. The town of Rotorua was created and the Domain of Te Aroha was set aside.

Bathhouses were built and the first medical position related to the mineral and geothermal waters was created. After Rolleston relinquished his folio, spa development slowed down, but the rapid progress during those 4 years generated considerable interest from the private sector.

The grandest scheme was proposed in 1884 by James Stewart, who was largely responsible for the initial stages of the railway to Rotorua. Some of Stewart's

The Pavilion Baths, Rotorua's original bathhouse, opened in 1882. William Deverell's illustration gives the spa an international flavour. From *The Hot Lakes Wonderland of New Zealand*, Brett, c. 1895. *Auckland Institute and Museum.*

proposals for the future of Rotorua indicate that he may have had some experience of European spas: "Both the hydropathic and Tourist branches of the establishment should be on a magnificent scale as regards amount and variety of accommodation . . . nothing less than the scale of a first class Continental Spa should be aimed at."[3] Stewart believed that the attractions of Rotorua could be made irresistible to European spa visitors and that the consequent influx of visitors would be very important to the colony. He considered that Whakarewarewa was the best site for the spa, with hotels on the ridge above the present Forestry Research Institute. The town would extend from the Tarawera Road to the Taupo Road. He also foresaw villas on the Owhata (Hinemoa's Point), Owhatiura, Koutu and Kawaha Point domes, overlooking the lake. Furthermore, he felt Rotorua could emulate the Italian spa of Acqui, where semitropical fruit and vegetables were ripened with geothermal heat. (Sixty years later Rotorua had similar hothouses.) A cable car was to connect the accommodation on the ridge with the bathhouses on the thermal flat. At the rear of the town, lit with electricity generated by the Puarenga Stream, Stewart envisaged a park extending over the Moerangi dome to the Green and Blue Lakes.

Had such a town been possible in the 1880s, it might well have attracted a European and American clientele. In reality, however, the resources of the country were insufficient for the project at that time, especially as New Zealand was going through a severe economic depression. The small-scale development initiated at Rotorua, Te Aroha and Hanmer may, in fact, have resulted from the need to attract capital to New Zealand. Unfortunately, there was not enough money available to make those areas attractive alternatives to spas in France or Germany.

Realising the need for more sophistication, the Government sent Camille Malfroy, the Custodian of the Rotorua Sanatorium, to report on European spas in 1891. Three years later, an English doctor publicised the country's hot spring resources in *New Zealand for the Emigrant*. Although the English writer added very little to what had already been printed, this British publicity given to New Zealand's spa potential was an encouragement to the colonial Government. At the end of 1897, the Government's representative in London, Agent-General William Pember Reeves, was asked to find a balneologist.

Reeves included a warning in his report on the European situation: "People who go to lounge or to gamble or to meet others of equal social status with themselves or — as is frequently the case — to flutter in the neighbourhood of social magnates, are not likely . . . to make voyages to the other end of the world."[4] Reeves had a difficult brief. He had been asked to find someone who, as well as being a physician and an analyst, had some knowledge of engineering and land-scaping — and who would accept a salary of £400. He eventually found a German spa specialist who would take the position at a salary of £1,000 — if he were allowed to accept private patients.

The Rotorua *Hot Lakes Chronicle* was not impressed: "We, of Maoriland, are not enamoured of articles made in Germany and would prefer an expert with a British hall-mark."[5] The German doctor was not accepted and the matter of the balneologist had to wait until 1902 after the Department of Tourist and Health Resorts had been set up.

Sir Joseph Ward, the first Minister of this new department, and Thomas Donne, its Superintendent and later General Manager, felt that Rotorua could be developed as an international spa. The other hot springs could be developed as secondary spas (Hanmer and Te Aroha) and small spas (such as Morere and Te Puia), which would become important nodes in tourist circuits. As soon as the department took office it began to search for a suitable balneologist. The successful candidate, Arthur Wohlmann of Bath, advised the Government to concentrate its tourist expenditure on "making a really first-class watering place". To develop all the potential spas would be too expensive, but one springs area should be "made so attractive that visitors from outside the country must be drawn . . . in ever-increasing numbers".[6]

Wohlmann believed that Rotorua was the place to be developed, advocating that it be made into a garden city, and that its architecture be strictly controlled. "There must," he wrote, "not only be decent comfort, but a certain amount of luxury."[7]

Concentrating development on Rotorua resulted in problems. Even before the Tourist Department was created there was constant criticism from other areas of the amount of money being invested in Rotorua. At a later stage the Rotorua

The Rotorua tea house and Bathhouse in about 1910 look almost like a spa in Edwardian England. *Photograph by Frank Radcliffe, Rotorua Museum.*

Bathhouse was opened before the building was completed, because of anxiety at the possible reaction of taxpayers to the cost of the structure. Although considerably more money was invested in Rotorua than in any other spa area, there was never quite enough spent to make it the garden oasis and cultural centre that Wohlmann envisaged.

On the one hand the Government was in a unique position to enforce certain architectural requirements; after 1890 it owned all the land in the Rotorua town area. On the other hand, it may well have felt that if it were too restrictive about building requirements it would never sell the leases. In fact, because Rotorua people were on 99-year leases, many leaseholders tended to erect very basic buildings (until 1920 when it became possible to purchase the freehold). Apart from the wide streets surveyed in 1881, and the plane trees planted along town streets in the 1890s, Rotorua resembled a dusty or muddy shanty town until the 1920s. (There were exceptions, of course: the Sanatorium Grounds which became the Government Gardens, the unique villages of Ohinemutu and Whakarewarewa, and a few handsome buildings such as the Rotorua Baths and the Grand Hotel.)

The other factor that defeated the plan to create an important spa in the South Pacific was technology. The Rotorua spa failed because of the enormous cost of maintenance. Nowhere in the world did another building have to survive such a difficult environment. Early this century there was no technology to cope with the highly acidic water used in the Bathhouse building and it was only 50 years later that polythene pipes were shown to be capable of conveying this water for

9

THE BLUE (SWIMMING) BATH.
ROTORUA.

Illustrations such as this, from a pictorial book of 1895, should have been incorporated in advertisements in Germany, Austria, France and the United States, as well as Britain; the people who visited spas in those countries did not have any knowledge of what New Zealand offered. From *The Hot Lakes Wonderland of New Zealand*, Brett, c. 1895. *Auckland Institute and Museum Library.*

long periods without disintegrating. If there had been sufficient money available to tile the entire interior walls, instead of plastering them, the building would not have come to look like a ruin. In fact, the whole New Zealand spa concept was doomed by the selection of wood plaster for the walls of the Rotorua Bathhouse. As the material rotted in the acidic atmosphere, so the department's interest in spas declined. By the 1920s most of the department's annual reports were devoted to the acclimatisation of deer, trout, pheasants and ducks. Encouraging hunters and fishermen had become more important than attracting visitors to bathe in Rotorua's hot waters.

The second wave of spa development in New Zealand, under the Tourist Department, suffered because the First World War followed so closely upon the opening of the Rotorua Bathhouse. The building had only 5 years of tourist patronage before the war brought a cut in public spending and a decline in receipts, with free bath treatment for soldiers. In 1908–09 the department spent £23,910 on capital works; in 1917, £967. During the 1920s there was considerable economic restraint, but, curiously, the last large-scale spa development took place during the Depression, as a result of Sir Joseph Ward's return to power.

10

Wherever you go . . .
However you go . . .

BOOKING AND ALL INFORMATION GOVERNMENT TOURIST BUREAU FENTON STREET—ROTORUA

Government Round Trip.
Geyserland's most fascinating tour. Rotorua, Earthquake Flats, Waimangu Geyser Valley, Simmering Lake Rotomahana by launch—an interesting walk—then Lake Tarawera by launch and a Service-car tour back via the scenic Blue and Green Lakes.

YOUR   PASSPORT
TO HEALTH AND
HAPPINESS IN ROTORUA

The Magnificent . . .

GOVERNMENT BATHS

SITUATED IN THE GOVERNMENT GARDENS

FOR PLEASURE . . .
THE FAMOUS BLUE BATHS
MIXED BATHING IN LIQUID LIGHT

White tiled . . . sparkling blue waters . . . submerged lighting . . . diving towers . . . sun balconies . . . richly furnished and carpeted rest room. Picture this and you have not a Hollywood conception, but a mental image of the peerless Blue Baths.

FOR HEALTH . . .
THE DUCHESS SWIMMING POOLS

For men and women—Ward Bath Buildings.

FOR MEN AND WOMEN . . .
RACHEL SWIMMING POOLS
Ward Bath Buildings

THE PRIEST BATH

Ward and Main Bath Buildings. "Old Priest," for nerves and heart. "New Priest," for Rheumatism and Debility. Most valuable allies in the treatment of Arthritis and cases of Debility.

MIRACULOUS MUD BATHS

Have a bland sedative effect of the tissues. For Neuritis and Gout.

Also latest Aix Massage and Electrical Baths and Treatments.

Facilities for Tennis, Croquet, Bowls and Golf are available in the Government Gardens, and PLAYING MATERIAL MAY BE HIRED.

Turn to page 6 of the Rotorua "Morning Post" for Government Baths Timetable or inquire at Bath Buildings.

There were not enough advertisements like this between 1885 and 1925, and not enough advertising overseas. *Rotorua Carnival Brochure*, 1936. *Rotorua Museum.*

Although he died in 1930 he had sought and received approval for new baths at Rotorua.

Even before the expensive Ward Baths and Blue Baths were completed, the department began to change its attitude towards spas, as can be seen in this letter written in 1931: "this Department has interests in more hot springs than it can find funds to adequately develop."[8] The last spa development carried out by the department was the addition, in 1965, of Aix massage to the Ward Baths. Six years later it withdrew from all connection with geothermal water.

Not surprisingly, the Government's outlook on spas had also changed. This was especially so after the Health Department took control of most of the thera-peutic functions at Rotorua. There the department has concentrated on the treat-ment of rheumatic and arthritic diseases, by the use of physiotherapy, splinting, drugs, remedial exercises and occupational therapy. The new attitude to spa waters was summed up by Dr Lennane, Director of Physical Medicine, in 1951:

> The use of Mineral Baths is now regarded as merely an adjuvant to these more effective measures, and it is not considered that any mineral waters applied externally or taken internally have a specific action on arthritis. The benefit gained by mineral baths is now considered to be due merely to heat and moisture, and with some waters, to a counter-irritant effect.[9]

This philosophy led to the development of the purely medical functions of hydro-therapy with the Queen Elizabeth Hospital at Rotorua, while, on the other hand, the Government lost interest in the fashionable tourist facilities of international spas.

By the 1960s the main symbol of the Tourist Department's effort to create a great spa in the Southern Hemisphere was a ruin; the Rotorua Bathhouse ceased to function as such in 1966. Distance from the clientele of the European spas, and the lack of population in the immediate vicinity worked against the project; extra-ordinary maintenance problems and a change of philosophy killed it.

References

1   Johnson, J. *Notes from a Journal Kept During an Excursion to the Boiling Springs of Rotorua and Rotomahana . . . in the summer of 1846 and 1847.*

2   Fox, the Hon. W. "Hot Springs district of the North Island" (letter to the Hon. the Premier). *Appendices to the Journal of the House of Representatives*, 1874, H–26.

3   Stewart, James. "On the establishment of a grand hotel and sanatorium in Rotorua district." Paper read at the Auckland Institute, 27 October 1884, Auckland, Wilson & Horton, 1884.

4   Reeves, William Pember. "Our thermal springs and their development." Memorandum for the Premier Richard Seddon, November 1897. Department of Lands and Survey file 35894/25.

5   *Hot Lakes Chronicle*, 14 May 1898.

6   Report of Government Balneologist. In *Appendices to the Journal of the House of Representatives*, 1903, H–2.

7   *Ibid.*

8   General Manager, Department of Tourist and Health Resorts, to Under Secretary, Department of Lands and Survey, 3 October 1931.

9   G. A. Q. Lennane, Director of Physical Medicine, to the Director–General of Health, 8 January 1951.

3 Waiwera — The First Spa

European spas often combined their mineral waters with attractive scenery — for example Buxton and Matlock in England's Derbyshire peak district or Evian and Aix-les-Bains in the Savoy Alps region of France. Waiwera (the name means, literally, hot water), 48 km north-west of Auckland, had this same advantage. In the 1870s, at a time when travellers to the Volcanic Plateau springs saw little but endless stretches of manuka scrub, Waiwera was an oasis of cultivation and comfort.

The springs, and the Maoris' use of them, were described as early as 1841:

> At the mouth of a creek about five miles south of Mahurangi the main spring gushes out from a high cliff, about two feet from its base; and successive jets, apparently from the same source, bubble up through the sand, along a line of about a hundred yards, from south to north, all covered at high water. Approaching the springs, the atmosphere is strongly impregnated with sulphur. The natives have recourse to these springs for the cure of different cutaneous disorders with which they are commonly affected. The cliff-spring is always accessible; the others only at low water. When any person wishes to bathe he digs himself a pool in the sand, sufficiently deep to allow of his lying down, lining it with branches to prevent the sand from refilling it. He may then enjoy a comfortable bath.[1]

The springs were known to the various tribes around the Hauraki Gulf as Te Rata — the Doctor. Bones on the beach at Waiwera were evidence of a battle for possession of this asset and Maoris from Coromandel frequently visited the springs for treatment.

In 1842 a Scottish businessman, Robert Graham, bought this area, having been fascinated by the sight of up to 3000 Maoris assembled on Waiwera's beach and bathing in holes in the sand. His lessee of the property advertised in 1848 that a house had been opened "for the accommodation of invalids, travellers and pleasure parties"[2] and a separate advertisement in the same paper announced that the cutter *Hot Springs* would sail for "Wai wera wera".

Bathing conditions at this time were recalled by the Auckland *Echo*: "a bath could only be obtained by digging out a hole in the sand on the beach, into which the water flowed, and the bather lying down stopped in it till the sand gradually filled in under him and left him lying on the beach again."[3]

Only when Robert Graham took over the administration of his property, in 1875, did Waiwera achieve considerable popularity. The hotel was extended, bathhouses were built and the water was bottled, and Graham advertised Waiwera Seltzer — "a medicinal, invigorating and cooling draught and purifier

13

Robert Graham's spa was built on a spit between the Waiwera River and the sheltered Hauraki Gulf. A storm, however, wrecked the stone bathhouse at the edge of the sea. *Alexander Turnbull Library.*

of the blood". Readers were also instructed to ask for Waiwera Tonic, described as "an unequalled stomachic and appetiser". These waters were "sold by respectable hotel-keepers"; Robert Graham owned hotels in Auckland, no doubt managed by "respectable hotel-keepers".[4]

When the water had been analysed in 1868,[5] the principal solids were found to be sodium chloride, magnesium chloride and sodium bicarbonate. In 1890 a visiting doctor explained that, "Used as a drinking spring the Waiwera water is not disagreeable, resembling diluted Wiesbaden water . . . it may be used as a preventive of calculus [formation of kidney stones] and to relieve acidity of the stomach."[6]

The source of the hot spring water was traced to the bottom of a cliff and a shaft was driven into the rock so that a reservoir could be filled to supply 18 private baths and a large plunge pool. There was also a bath just above high water mark, reached by waves in stormy weather. Jacob Multrus, one of the Puhoi Bohemians, made this bath out of natural rock and mortar, although photographs show that the stone was replaced by brick, and, eventually, by weatherboard. Sulphur from White Island was added to some baths to provide an artificial equivalent of some of the Rotorua waters. An 1878 Waiwera pamphlet

14

claimed that these particular baths were "equal, with superior local advantages, to those already so highly prized in other parts of the Island".[7] It was, of course, referring to the acidic baths at Sulphur Point in Rotorua. The claim avoided the point that anyone could shovel sulphur into their own domestic bath.

Robert Graham published advice and painted notice boards for his boarders: "Take a bath before breakfast, a second in the afternoon, and a third before going to rest at night, drinking a cupful of the mineral water before and after each bath."[8] He gave a glowing description of his hotel accommodation: "the table is abundantly supplied with every delicacy of the season to tempt the appetite of the invalid, as well as the robust."[9]

As in European spas, attention was given to the entertainment of guests: "Everything is conducted in a regular and methodical manner. Meals are always ready at the appointed hours; and pleasant cheerful company, chess, drafts, billiards, whist, music, croquet, lawn tennis, and other games afford a variety of amusement, and effectually dispel monotony."[10] At this stage, 1878, the hotel was superior to anything on the Volcanic Plateau.

In fact, newspapers at the time were "emphatic in their enconiums", as the *New Zealand Herald* put it on 13 September 1875, and Waiwera came in for much praise and was widely recommended, even for those patients "who are not blessed with a plethora of cash".[11] Author William Senior described the hotel as "probably the largest in New Zealand" in 1880, and praised it for being "fitted up with liberal means of recreation, and extra comforts worthy of a first rate English watering place". He specially admired Robert Graham's sister as being "able to keep even querulous old gentlemen and peevish ladies . . . from quarrelling."[12]

Waiwera was noted for its unique travel arrangements. Most visitors arrived by small steamship from Auckland, but as there was no wharf until 1905, and since the spa was situated in a shallow bay, the tourists and invalids had to put ashore by ships' boats. This experience was described by Mrs Charles Dudley Robert Ward, writing under the pseudonym of Thorpe Talbot for her *New Guide to the Lakes and Hot Springs, and a month in hot water*, 1882:

> The landing at Waiwera is a comical affair . . . At present the method is for the steamer to run in as near shore as possible, cast anchor, and send her passengers and cargo off in boats. The boats, in turn, run as near the shore as is possible for them, and are met by a horse and cart . . . It was the first time I had been at sea in a carriage, and the sensation was unique.[13]

Once ashore, visitors were almost invariably impressed by Waiwera's pleasant surroundings. The bay was a complete contrast to the stark atmosphere of the Sulphur Point area at Rotorua where baths were being established in 1882. There were willow, poplar and eucalyptus trees, an avenue of pines and flower and strawberry beds. Peacocks wandered through the peaceful, scented gardens. Adding to the atmosphere of the place, especially in summer, were the many courting couples, no doubt chaperoned, whose presence gave Waiwera something of a European spa air of trysts and assignations.

Mrs Ward also left us interesting details about the actual bathing. A walk through the avenue of pines took bathers to a series of small apartments fitted up with wooden or tiled bathtubs. "Two obliging attendants are always at hand with an abundance of clean towels and anything else you may happen to want. That liberality with the towels is in itself a charmful thing to anyone who has 'lived about' and experienced the economy generally displayed in such matters."[14]

The temperature of the water ranged from 37.8 to 43.3°C, and Mrs Ward warned that "if you plump yourself in rather suddenly . . . your first idea is that you are permanently cooked and done for".[15] Apart from slow immersion, she advised the use of a cool, damp towel for the head. Visitors then showered, rubbed themselves with coarse towels, returned to the hotel and slept away the languor induced by the hot water. (No doubt the use of very hot water produced the occasional stroke.)

Like William Senior before her, Mrs Ward was impressed with the hostess, Miss Graham, whom she described as "in her portly, vigorous, healthful self, calculated to make one ashamed of being an invalid, and anxious to throw off the merest suspicion of weakness". In the author's opinion, Miss Graham should have been a man and a general, "Not that she is lacking in womanly tenderness and sympathy . . . but she is such a splendid disciplinarian and tactician".[16]

Another important feature of the attraction of Waiwera was its mild and pleasant climate. It is sheltered by hills to the south, west and north, while to the east is the peninsula- and island-protected Hauraki Gulf.

Also vital to Waiwera's success was Miss Graham's organisation of recreation; she made certain her patients did not suffer from boredom. (In Rotorua, at a later stage, the Government-appointed Balneologist was to warn the Tourist Department that they must do all in their power to prevent ennui among the Rotorua bathers.) Unfortunately, the entertainments offered at this "Brighton of New Zealand",[17] as Robert Graham called it, included shooting kaka and picking up human bones (the remnants of a battle) from the beach. Tourists were also recommended to visit a nearby Maori village and the Bohemian settlers at Puhoi, and to collect ferns from the bush.

After all the praise from the papers, periodicals and brochures, it is something of a relief to discover from one traveller that the place wasn't all as sweet as the strawberries and cream Miss Graham was wont to serve. In his 1888 *Round About New Zealand*, the artist, photographer and first director of Elam School of Art, E. W. Payton was bluntly realistic about the means of transport to Waiwera: "The road is what is known as a 'summer road'; that is, it consists almost altogether of mud."[18] He had, too, an unusually rough passage from Auckland to Waiwera:

> No one would believe how soon a big sea can get up amongst these little islands. For three and a half hours we had as rough and uncomfortable a journey as I ever remember — seas constantly washing over the little craft, shaking her from stem to stern, and the screw half the time out of the water, tearing round and shaking the boat most uncomfortably . . . The gale increased in fury, and a heavy sea struck the little boat with such force that the passengers thought she was going down, and some commenced to take off their clothes to prepare for a swim.[19]

The ship's boats were swamped, an occurrence that Archibald Sutter had claimed in 1887 was not infrequent. Mary Bilman described another shortcoming of the day trips from Auckland to Waiwera at the turn of the century: "The steamer

Waiwera, about 1885. This was the method of landing at the spa until 1905 when a very long jetty was built from the shallow bay. *Photograph by Burton Bros, National Museum.*

would arrive about mid-day, bringing 300–400 excursionists. By the time all had been landed it was nearly time to start loading again, and the last off the boat would probably only have been ashore a quarter of an hour before three blasts from the ship announced it was time to start moving."[20]

When the Waiwera estate came up for sale in 1908 the inventory of property would have impressed one of Galsworthy's Forsytes. There were 270 ha, freehold, with sea frontages and the Waiwera River. Eighty ha were in grass, the remainder in native forest. There was a jetty and a boathouse on the river. As well as good fishing and pheasant shooting, there were 2 croquet lawns, a bowling green and 3 tennis courts (with a choice of hard and grass surface). There were 1.6 ha of orchard and kitchen garden, a social hall, a billiard parlour, a bar and a store. As well as stables, dairy, laundry and so on, there were 8 furnished cottages. The kauri hotel had 50 bedrooms, 2 drawing rooms, a smoking room, a card room, a coffee room, a dining room and a children's dining room.

The bathing inventory included "a large Gentlemen's Hot-water Swimming Bath", which refilled itself when emptied, the springs being "all over the floor". The private bathhouse contained 2 waiting rooms and 15 bathrooms. At the end of this building was "a large Ladies Hot-water Swimming Bath",[21] supplied by

Waiwera had a great reputation for the rest cure. The hotel was destroyed by fire in 1939. *Photograph by Muir and Moodie, National Museum.*

the spring in the cliff. Early this century the Government twice declined an offer to purchase all or part of the estate, and without the Grahams, the original spa gradually declined, especially after the old hotel was destroyed by fire in 1939.

Possibly because many bores were installed in the 1950s and 1960s, but also because of sea water infiltrating the hot water aquifer, the natural springs ceased to flow during the 1960s. The first pool of the present Waiwera complex opened at the end of 1957, Hartley Hot Pools being several 100 m from the original hot springs area. Using bore water and an ozone plant, the complex offers 8 outdoor pools, a large indoor pool, 19 private pools, children's pools, party and barbecue facilities and, since 1978, stainless steel water chutes and choobs. Waiwera is an important recreational area for Auckland but looks fairly similar to other large aquatic centres throughout New Zealand. While there are places at Rotorua and Te Aroha where the visitor can sense the atmosphere of an Edwardian spa, this is unlikely to be the case at Waiwera. Everything belongs very firmly to the twentieth century.

References

1   "A Journal in New Zealand" in *Madras Protestant Guardian*, 1841.
2   *New Zealander*, 12 December 1848.
3   *Echo*, 20 July 1875.
4   *Auckland Weekly News*, 9 February 1877.
5   "Proceedings of the Auckland Institute" in *Transactions of the New Zealand Institute*, 1868, p. 476.
6   Moore, J. *New Zealand for the Emigrant, Invalid and Tourist*, Sampson Low, 1890.
7   *Waiwera Hot Springs, the Sanitarium of New Zealand and the Australian Colonies*, Auckland, Herald, 1878.
8   Wilson, A. *Maoriland, an illustrated handbook of New Zealand*, Wellington, Union S.S. Co., 1884.
9   *Waiwera Hot Springs Sanitarium, near Auckland, New Zealand*, Auckland Herald [1875].
10 *Waiwera Hot Springs, the Sanitarium of New Zealand . . . op. cit.*
11 *New Zealand Herald*, 13 September 1875.
12 Senior, William. *Travel and Trout in the Antipodes*, London, Chatto & Windus, 1880.
13 Talbot, Thorpe [pseudonym for Mrs Charles Dudley Robert Ward]. *The New Guide to the Lakes and Hot Springs, and a month in hot water*, Wilson & Horton, 1882.
14 *Ibid.*
15 *Ibid.*
16 *Ibid.*
17 Graham, Robert Jnr. *Graham's Guide to the Hot Lakes of New Zealand, Pink and White Terraces, Wairakei Geysers, Huka Falls and Waiwera Hot Springs*, Auckland, Wilson & Horton, 1884.
18 Payton, E. W. *Round About New Zealand. Being notes from a journal of three years wanderings in the Antipodes*, London, Chapman & Hall, 1888.
19 *Ibid.*
20 Bilman, Mary. *A Century in Hot Water, a tale of Waiwera*, Warkworth, The Rodney and Waitemata Times, 1965.
21 Mowbray, W. R., Estate Agent, Shortland Street, Auckland. For sale description: The Waiwera hot springs estate and hotel, March 1908. Tourist Department file 1901/148.

4 Rotorua 1870–1901

For most of the last century Rotorua has been New Zealand's main tourism centre and for the first half of that period the principal attraction was geothermal activity, especially bathing in mineral water, either for pleasure or for medicinal purposes.

Large numbers of tourists arrived on the Plateau after fighting, against Hauhau groups in 1867 and against Te Kooti in 1870, had ceased. Many of the early travellers came for one purpose — to see the "eighth wonder of the world", the Pink and White Terraces at Rotomahana. While in the Rotorua area most of the visitors tried the baths. Before 1870 European travellers bathed at Ohinemutu, but from then onwards an increasing number bathed in the area now known as the Government Gardens.

This area, originally called Oruawhata, came to be known as Sulphur Point. From 1886, for approximately 30 years, the place was called the Sanatorium Grounds and, since then, has become the Government Gardens. Until 1882 the Sulphur Point area was a wasteland of sinter, sulphur and manuka, described by one observer as a "howling wilderness".[1]

Most of the thermal activity was concentrated at the edge of the lake, a place described on maps as Te Kauwhanga, although the name was probably Te Kauanga — the resting place for canoes. In contrast to the brown mudpools and acidic yellow waters of Te Kauanga, there were 2 beautiful blue chloride pools to the west of the lake. Oruawhata pool has now disappeared. Probably only Europeans used the bath made from this spring, as a Maori child had been scalded to death in the source, rendering it tapu. The other pool, originally known as Whangapipiro, was rechristened Madam Rachel, after a London cosmetician who claimed "to make the plain pretty, to make beautiful exquisite, and to make the age of golden youth eternal".[2] She was jailed for fraud; and like her preparations, the pool's effects are only temporary, a deposit of silica making the bather's skin unusually smooth. Rachel water became famous, however, for its quality of coating any surface.

Most bathers tried the pool of sulphury water south of Te Kauanga known, after the apparent cure of a Catholic priest, as the Priest's Bath. In 1878 Father Mahoney of Tauranga, crippled with arthritis, was carried to Rotorua. After a considerable amount of immersion in the acidic waters of the pool he was able to walk back to Tauranga. This waiariki, or spring used for bathing, was recalled by Rotorua's first Resident Medical Officer as "a small hole in the rough pumice formation on the beach of Lake Rotorua, with a manuka breakwind. The bath

20

would just hold four people tightly packed".[3] Such bathers travelled great distances to this pool which, to some extent, became New Zealand's Bethesda. Its original name was Te Pupunitanga and it had been used by the Arawa people for centuries.

Thomas Hope Lewis, the Medical Officer, in his 1885 *Medical Guide to the Mineral Waters of Rotorua*, listed several remarkable improvements to invalids bathing in the Priest's Bath and other pools in the area,[4] but his successor, Alfred Ginders, warned against doctors sending incurable patients to Rotorua.[5]

From 1880 to 1900 many of the natural pools were used for bathing. In some cases, however, the springs themselves were too hot and so a channel had to be dug a sufficient distance from the source for the water to be bearable. A contemporary print showed men up to their shoulders in these small artificial pools, looking like some of the denizens of Dante's Hell.

Many of the natural pools were named after settlers or visitors who used them regularly. Cameron's Bath at Te Kauanga was alternatively named the White Sulphur Bath and the Laughing Gas Pool, the third title referring to the effects of hydrogen sulphide emitted from the surface, effects similar to the reaction to dentists' nitrous oxide.

An 1879 visitor, Clement Bunbury, wrote of bathing in "waves of thick brown mud".[6] At the Coffee Pot pool bathers tied a rope between manuka bushes and suspended themselves in dark brown liquid. South of the Priest's Bath was a spring named Toko. This was the name given to Rotorua's first Postmaster, Roger Dansey, who used that spring. He also wrote one of the best descriptions of the 1886 Tarawera eruption.

The Priest's Bath area was the site of the first Government bathhouse in the country. It opened in 1882 but had to be rebuilt 2 years later as acidic steam had corroded the nails. "Yesterday," said the *Auckland Weekly News* in April 1883, "the bottom fell out of one of the Government baths, leaving Mr Carter, the famous coach proprietor of Cambridge, high and dry among the debris."[7]

Originally known as the bath pavilion, the building in front of the Priest Bath came to be known as the Pavilion Baths. From 1884 to 1887 the Priest Baths were open air pools with awnings and dressing boxes. Within the main pavilion structure Rachel baths were available. For several years, however, there were no showers in the bathhouse and women's skins particularly became red and irritated if the acidic water was not removed within a short time. As against the pleasant effect of the Rachel water, containing sodium chloride and sodium silicate as its main salts, the principal constituent in the Priest water is sulphuric acid.

On the women's side of the pavilion, the cubicles or "apartments", as the 1884 Union Steamship Company's guide book described them, contained 2 baths. According to the guide this was "so that the pleasures of society and conversation can be combined with the luxury of immersion in the hot mineral water".[8]

The most outstanding writer to visit Rotorua at this time was the English historian and philosopher, James Anthony Froude who, in 1885, considered the future of the bathing area in his *Oceana*: "This desert promontory — Sulphur

The Pavilion Baths, Rotorua. This was the first Government bathhouse. The men are bathing in a piscine (the Roman name for a sunken rectangular bath). *Rotorua Museum.*

Point — with its sad green lake and Maori huts and distant smoke columns, will hereafter be an enormous cockney watering place: and here it will be that in some sanitarium salon Macaulay's New Zealander, returning from his travels will exhibit his sketch of the ruins of St Paul's to groups of admiring ladies".[9] Thus Froude expressed his faith in the future of the Rotorua spa, continuing after the collapse of London.[10] The Rotorua description was more poetic than accurate; there were no Maori huts at Sulphur Point in 1885 and the smoke columns were undoubtedly columns of steam.

Less poetic were the various lists of complaints that doctors thought might benefit from the waters at Sulphur Point. Dr Hope Lewis advised the Priest water for a great number of ailments including sexual impotence and he used Oruawhata water to kill slugs and snails.[11] Dr Ginders claimed that the Rotorua waters "reduce plethora and corpulency without prostration",[12] while in 1887 the Inspector of Hospitals considered that Rotorua was a place "of refuge" for persons who suffered from congestions of various "viscera".[13]

There is some mystery over the hospital which was built near the bath pavilion, to serve partly as a sanatorium for invalids using the baths. Construction began in 1883, and it was substantially completed during 1884, yet it did not open until December 1885. The economic depression the country was going through was most likely responsible for the delay. It was not a large institution, accommodating just 12 patients. The administration of the hospital was curious also. Dr Ginders was responsible only for medical attention; all the administration of the building was in the hands of Dunbar Johnson, the town's Government Agent.

The first Rotorua hospital or sanatorium 1885–88. The administration of this building was divided between the Department of Lands and Survey and the Hospitals and Charities Department. *Rotorua Museum.*

A French engineer from the West Coast of the South Island was given a new Government position after the 1886 Tarawera disaster. One of Camille Malfroy's duties was to keep an eye on changes in thermal activity, in case there was another eruption, but, as Overseer of Works, much of his activity related to the baths. He built a proper bathhouse over the Priest pools, provided the pavilion with a wooden clock which was not affected by the acidic steam, and installed hot water douches or jets for bathers. A reporter for Rotorua's *Hot Lakes Chronicle* was particularly satisfied with the last device, in 1887: "I found a poor sufferer directing the stream by his own hand to whatever part he desired. The effect appeared to be most beneficial and delightful, judging from the ecstatic manner in which he handled the invention."[14]

The Priest Bathhouse was built almost entirely without nails. The difficulty of providing durable materials in Rotorua was outlined by Margaret Bullock in her *The World's Sanatorium*, 1897:

> the waters . . . in a very short time, rot and destroy every substance left in contact with them . . . Iron rusts, wood rots, stone crumbles under the action of the strong acids with which the waters are charged. The conduit pipes are quickly filled up by silica deposits, and no roofing has yet been found proof against the destructive action of the ascending vapours. Mineral coatings pattern the walls of the baths, the floors of the dressing rooms, and every surface to which water or steam gets access . . .[15]

Margaret Bullock was not sympathetic with the views of some travellers renewing acquaintance with the Rotorua area in the last years of the nineteenth

Rotorua c. 1886. In the foreground is the Oruawhata pool which supplied the original Blue Baths (at left). At the rear are the distant buildings of Brent's Hotel, the Native Hospital and the first Sanatorium (1885–88). *Auckland Institute and Museum.*

century. They recalled with nostalgia the pre-bathhouse days, but she considered that conditions before 1882 were especially difficult for women bathers "when the manuka fringing the various curative springs afforded the invalid an indifferent screen from possible observation, but no protection whatever from the weather".[16]

Those who objected to the replacement of manuka bush with weatherboards would have noted a proliferation of buildings on Froude's "desert promontory". The natural bath filled from the Oruawhata spring had been replaced with a simple wooden bathhouse, the Blue Bath, opened by the English journalist George Augustus Sala in 1885. Dressing boxes and a small bath were provided at the Painkiller Pool. A women's swimming bath was added on to the Pavilion Baths in 1896. Before that, with only a few hours allotted to women's bathing at the Blue Bath per week, it seemed that the authorities did not consider swimming a suitable occupation for women.

Baths of very acidic water were opened in 1895 near the Toko spring, on a peculiarly depressing site south of the Sanatorium Grounds. Another Post Office official, from Wellington, had bathed here, so the bathhouse became known as the Postmaster's Bath. Because so much hydrogen sulphide emanated from these baths, they had to be left open to the atmosphere. Even so, there were still cases, as Dr Ginders reported, of "fainting and involuntary muscular twitching, without loss of consciousness, among men using these baths. The women appear to enjoy a singular immunity from these troubles".[17] Dr Ginders had a curious belief that bathing in this very acidic water reduced the craving for alcohol, a

Rotorua's original swimming bath. Designed by the Tauranga architect, Arthur Washington Burrows, and fed from the natural hot pool, Oruawhata, it was opened by the London journalist, George Augustus Sala, in 1885. The building was demolished in 1931. *Photograph by Sidney Vaile, Auckland Institute and Museum.*

suggestion that amused Samuel Clemens, better known to us as Mark Twain, when he wrote his *More Tramps Abroad*, published in 1900.[18]

After the Tarawera eruption in June 1886, the famous Te Wairoa tohunga, Tuhoto, was taken to the Sanatorium. Reputed to be more than 100 years old, he was excavated from the eruption mud after 104 hours underground. At the Sanatorium the old tohunga's hair was cut because it was matted with volcanic debris. He died a few days later, some said because tapu had been violated when his head was shorn.

The original hospital and Sanatorium burned down in November 1888. The bell rope was snapped off during attempts to summon help and the firefighting appliances were ineffective. The replacement Sanatorium was supplied with tanks of water so that the place could be drenched in an instant.

When the new building opened in 1890 the *Bay of Plenty Times* reported that "the officials are attentive and are under the direct influence of the matron, Miss Birch, who has the control of the internal comforts . . . and is a strict disciplinarian."[19] The Sanatorium was controlled, in turn, by the Lands and Survey Department, the Colonial Secretary's Department (this became the Department of Internal Affairs), the Lunacy Department and the Railways Department.

When Alfred Ginders retired, his replacement, Dr George Kenny, was responsible to the Railways Department, while Camille Malfroy's successor as Inspector of Works was an officer of the Lands and Survey Department. As the new Inspector, B. S. Corlett, was responsible for new works for the baths, the situation of 2

The women's open air pool at Rotorua's Pavilion Baths was opened in 1896. Before that an 1885 swimming bath was for men only. The costumes were probably worn only for the photographer's visit. *Auckland Institute and Museum.*

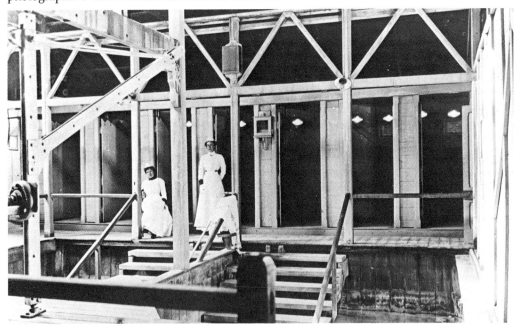

Rotorua's Pavilion Baths photographed about 1900, showing the Priest Baths and the Railways Department hoist used to lower and withdraw partially immobilised patients. It was capable of suspending 20 stone weights. *Canterbury Public Library.*

officers having different directors, and being involved in the administration of the same buildings was bound to create friction. It was to end only with the creation of a new department which would look after everything to do with the baths.

Even before the Department of Tourist and Health Resorts came into existence in 1901 the Government had been busy with some of the aspects that the new department would consider necessary for a spa. The town was made more attractive. Plane trees were planted along the verges of the main roads, while in the Sanatorium Grounds top soil was spread over the sinter and gardens were begun. The grounds were illuminated on summer nights, bands played on the verandah of the Sanatorium and artificial geysers amused strollers walking from the baths to the magnificent Grand Hotel, which provided comfort for wealthy visitors to the Rotorua spa.

References

1   Ginders, A. *The Thermal Springs District and the Government Sanatorium at Rotorua*, Wellington, Government Printer, 1897.
2   "Come into my beauty parlour" in *Headlines* magazine, June 1975.
3   Lewis, T. Hope. "The Thermal Waters of New Zealand" in *Cook's New Zealand Guide*, 5th ed., 1905.
4   Lewis, T. Hope. *Medical Guide to the Mineral Waters of Rotorua*, Auckland, Brett, 1885.
5   Ginders, Alfred. *The Thermal Springs, Rotorua, New Zealand, hints on cases likely to benefit by treatment thereat*, Wellington, Government Printer, 1885.
6   Bunbury, Clement. "A Visit to the New Zealand Geysers" in *Fraser's Magazine*, 1879.
7   *Auckland Weekly News*, 14 April 1883.
8   Wilson, A. *Maoriland, an illustrated handbook of New Zealand*, Wellington, Union S.S. Co., 1884.
9   Froude, James Anthony. *Oceana or England and her colonies*, London, Longmans, 1885.
10   The reference is to Macaulay's essay on von Ranke's history of the Popes. The image of a New Zealander returning to his country with an illustration of the ruins of St Pauls indicates the endurance of Rome, i.e. in such future time the church would still flourish.
11   Lewis, T. Hope. *Medical Guide to the Mineral Waters of Rotorua*, Auckland, Brett, 1885.
12   Ginders, Alfred. *The Thermal Springs District and the Government Sanatorium at Rotorua*, Wellington, Government Printer, 1897.
13   Inspector of Hospitals, Rotorua report 18 November 1886. *Appendices to the Journal of the House of Representatives*, 1887, H-19.
14   *Hot Lakes Chronicle*, 3 December 1887.
15   Bullock, Margaret. *The World's Sanatorium. A sketch of Rotorua and its environs*, Wellington, Government Printer, 1897.
16   *Ibid.*
17   Ginders, Alfred. *The Thermal Springs District and the Government Sanatorium at Rotorua*, Wellington, Government Printer, 1897.
18   Twain, Mark. *More Tramps Abroad.*
19   *Bay of Plenty Times*, 27 March 1893.

5 The Rotorua Baths

Known for the past 20 years as Tudor Towers, the Rotorua Bathhouse is both one of the most impressive symbols of the Tourist Department's work and a monument to the development of spas in New Zealand.

Credit is certainly due to the Tourist Department for most of the improvements to Rotorua's geothermal bathing facilities, but the pioneering work was done by the Lands and Survey Department, which was last involved with hot springs when it built the Duchess Bath, created for the visit of the Duke and Duchess of York and Cornwall in 1901. (The Duchess opened the bath but declined to take the waters.) The new bath was made because of embarrassment at the condition of the Pavilion Baths which, despite rebuilding, were suffering from "the vapours".

A private bathroom and dressing room at the Duchess Bath c. 1910. *Alexander Turnbull Library.*

The Duchess Bath at Rotorua, about 1910. This bathhouse, built for the visit of the Duke and Duchess of York and Cornwall in 1901, was replaced by the Ward Baths in 1929–30. *Auckland Institute and Museum.*

The idea of having a balneologist had been proposed before the Department of Tourist and Health Resorts was set up, but the new department made the position attractive enough to draw applications from European specialists. An English doctor, Arthur Stanley Wohlmann, was selected. At the time of his appointment he was working in the Royal Hospital at Bath, an institution specialising in rheumatic conditions. As part of his new work he visited the spas of Europe, so that when he reached New Zealand in July 1902 he had the experience to suggest changes to the Rotorua situation. As his superior, Thomas E. Donne, put it in 1902: "Dr Wohlmann is very anxious at once to proceed with the inauguration of a new era of things".[1] The new era included his residence. Wohlmann refused to install his good furniture in the borer-ridden Medical Officer's house, so a Balneologists's house was built.

The Balneologist was particularly keen to have a new bathhouse. The fact that electricity had been available in Rotorua since May 1901 meant that it would be easy to pump waters to any chosen site, so a new bathhouse would not be dependent upon the rise and fall of the lake, as was the case with the Priest Bath, built over a spring close to the edge of the lake. If the new building were placed on high ground it would be easy to empty the baths by gravitation.

Plans for the new bathhouse were begun in 1903 but the building didn't open until the second half of 1908. Dr Wohlmann was keen to introduce new treatment, so mudbaths were given in a lean-to structure at the back of the Priest Bath, and a small building at the rear of the Duchess Bath provided what was known as Aix massage, based upon the system used at the French spa of Aix-les-Bains.

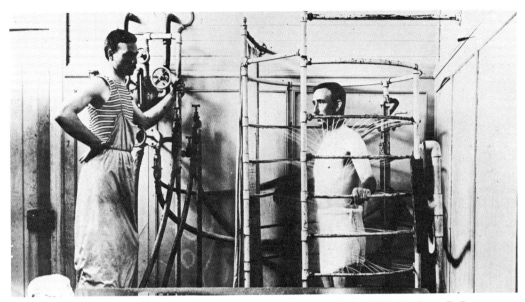

The Needle Douche in the massage unit behind the Duchess Bath, 1903–08. *From Railways Department Album, Alexander Turnbull Library.*

Apart from the fact that they provided treatments that weren't previously available, Wohlmann considered these temporary measures necessary because: "I should be ashamed utterly to prescribe any of the present baths to patients . . . I found the Priest Baths more like pig-stys than places for Christians to bathe in".[2]

Wohlmann also suggested the development of a hydro, which would be like the Sanatorium but on a grander scale. Whereas the Sanatorium provided mainly free accommodation for selected patients who could not afford to stay at Rotorua's hotels while receiving bath treatment, a hydro would be for wealthy patients — "a paying hospital run on comfortable modern lines".[3] Already committed to a new bathhouse, the Government did not want to be involved in the expense of another large Rotorua building. Had the hydro been built, however, Rotorua would have had a special atmosphere more like that of the European spas and would have attracted some of their clientele.

The Balneologist did not, however, think the European spas were a perfect model for Rotorua's bathhouse, with their "wealth of beautiful but chill-suggestive marble". There was, he considered, more comfort in the "homely timbered buildings of Nauheim [near Frankfurt] than in all the cold glory of marble palaces".[4] Accordingly, the Rotorua bathhouse was planned and completed as a timbered building. There was no suitable building stone near Rotorua, and Wohlmann felt it was better not to "try and make it look like stone by building in a pseudo-classic style". He therefore chose "the old English style of architecture, modified to meet modern Colonial requirements".[5] An essential feature of his plan was a central hall which would serve both as a meeting place and a waiting room "with comfortable lounges amongst ferns and growing flowers".

30

Presenting the building as though it might be found at Leamington or Woodhall Spa, this 1907 watercolour of the projected Rotorua Bathhouse emphasises the influence of British and European spas on the New Zealand Government's attempt to create an international spa at Rotorua. The wings of the bathhouse were intended to project beyond the transepts and patients in wheelchairs were to be admitted through side doors. *National Archives.*

Here people would drink mineral waters "of which I would have a variety on tap".[6]

B. S. Corlett, the Inspector of Works for the department, W. J. Trigg, the department's draughtsman, and J. W. Wrigley, a Rotorua architect, were responsible for the plans. Pumice concrete was used between the heart rimu timbers, totara for the main beams and kauri for the doors and wainscoting. The building was constructed on concrete arches 1.8 m high to allow easy access to pipes and drains. So that the bathhouse would not look as though it were built on stilts, an earth terrace was built up to floor level at the front of the building. The builders could not excavate for the foundations because of the probability of high concentrations of hydrogen sulphide beneath the surface.

The completed bathhouse was to have 14 deep, 42 shallow, 12 mud, 4 electrical, 8 massage-douche and 4 local vapour baths. Wohlmann believed he would be able to accommodate 1000 bathers a day, as well as giving 5 sunbaths and 10 inhalations at a time. There were difficulties with the planning. Dr Wohlmann wanted (and got) long, broad verandahs where visitors could promenade. He no doubt had in mind the area around the Pump Room at Bath, where people paraded to be seen, before or after drinking the waters. Corlett, on the other hand, as main architect for the building, felt it was not correct to have a verandah on a Tudor-style building.

Mr W. E. Hutchison of Auckland won the building contract with his tender of £25,720 and construction began in January 1906. The building was opened on 13

The Rotorua Bathhouse in 1909. Because of criticism of costs, the building was opened before it was complete; women had to use the unfinished wing. One transept was added to this in 1911, and a second by the Rotorua District Council in 1982. Apart from the asymmetry, it is the verandah and Gothic turret additions which give the building its unusual appearance. *Photograph by Muir and Moodie, Rotorua Museum.*

August 1908, before it was completed, by Admiral Sperry of the American Atlantic Fleet and Sir Joseph Ward. At the end of the year, when the fittings were installed, the Rotorua Bathhouse had cost £40,000. At this stage, however, the Superintendent of the Tourist and Health Resorts Department was able to persuade the Government that a stream of travellers would be attracted to the country by the new building. Alas, it was no Taj Mahal.

The Tourist Department also attempted to make Rotorua and the gardens attractive. The tea house opened in the grounds, now known as the Government Gardens, became the social centre of Rotorua. A band rotunda was built and bowling and croquet greens and tennis courts were added. In the town metal was spread on the pumice roads. (During the 1890s dust storms from the dry roads were sometimes so unpleasant that tourists would not leave their hotels. Snoods, veils or scarves were de rigeur for women travellers on the Plateau.)

Dr Wohlmann regretted that a casino could not be installed in the bathhouse; many wealthy visitors to the spas of Europe were partly attracted by the opportunity to gamble. Wohlmann emphasised the importance of social life in the bathhouse, as the centre of the Rotorua spa. The entrance hall became the equivalent of the English spa's pump room or the German kursaal, a place to shelter in bad weather, to listen to light music and to rendezvous in the evening. The doctor

The Rotorua Bathhouse foyer in July 1908. The Government Balneologist hoped that this area would serve the same social purpose as the pumproom of an English spa or the kursaal in a German establishment. *Rotorua Museum.*

felt a harp, violin and cornet would be sufficient for background music to begin with, although this combination seems rather a bizarre one for the sugary harmonies of the Edwardian salon repertoire. Dr Wohlmann laid great importance upon music: "no other single means will go so far to dispel the ennui of enforced idleness".[7] An aviary and monkey house were installed in the gardens and a camera obscura was built on a games-ticket office in the grounds, its kaleidoscopic effects no doubt emphasising the cultured retreat atmosphere of the Edwardian spa.

Some of the fittings in the bathhouse were unusual and, in some cases, unique. Foremost were 13 marble sculptures by Charles Francis Summers, an Australian sculptor who had lived in Rome. The bath cubicles were wainscoted in Minton porcelain tiles, and provided with plush-upholstered couches and nickle-plated handrails. The mudbath section boasted magnificent Royal Doulton porcelain baths.

Among the many types of treatments provided in the Rotorua Bathhouse was radium water, fresh water activated by exposure to radium bromide. Available for a few years from 1913, by the 1920s it had run out of emanations. This treatment seems very strange today in the light of our knowledge of radiation and its dangers. The water was supposed to reduce blood pressure and diminish the sugar in certain forms of diabetes. In large doses it acted as a purgative, and it had the unique property, according to a newspaper article, of tightening loose teeth.

33

Dr Shnee's electric four cell bath, used in the Rotorua Bathhouse, was supposed to increase the flow of blood to the extremities and it created involuntary movements of arthritic limbs. *National Archives*.

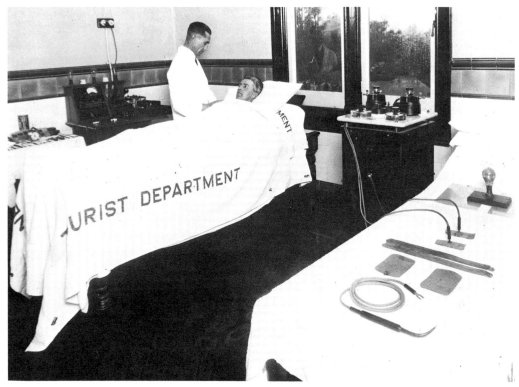

In the Rotorua Bathhouse in about 1927 Mr H. Croker, the head physiotherapist, is applying the dry Farado electric massage and diathermy. *From Railways Department Album, Alexander Turnbull Library.*

Another device was the Greville hot air bath in which a limb was exposed to intense dry heat from electric wires. Apparently parts of the body could be exposed to temperatures as high as 260°C without discomfort. It was particularly effective for stiff knees. In the Electric Light Bath the patient sat in a cabinet bathed in the glow of 50 incandescent and 4 arc lights. Most of the treatments, however, were Priest and Rachel baths and massages.

It was difficult to keep up with the demand for treatments because the women's end of the building was never completed. Massage for women was provided in a boarded-in verandah. The Plombiere douche, described by one doctor as "colonic irrigation", was unused for years because, until 1930, there was no suitable place in which to administer this treatment.

Entertainment was a problem too. The *Dominion* in 1911 complained of "a distressful piccolo" in the pump room and the Rotorua *Chronicle* lamented "a lame piano"[9] at the tearooms. Worse, claimed the newspaper article, "the breakdown (of the piano) is of an assertive character, causing complaints loud and long from the sufferer".[10] One of the conditions in a contract drawn up with an orchestra was that no piece of music was to be played more than twice in the same week, except by special request, and then only subject to the Balneologist's approval.

One of the tenders for the position of orchestra to the Government Gardens came from the splendidly titled Royal Symphony Orchestra of Arawa Street.

As Balneologist, Dr Wohlmann wrote 2 publications. The first, *The Mineral Waters and Health Resorts of New Zealand*, published in 1904, was a popular account of geothermal and mineral waters, while the second, *Mineral Waters and Spas of New Zealand*, was written in 1912 for the medical profession. After returning to Britain in 1919 he combined the 2 approaches in his 1921 *The Hot Springs of New Zealand*, and added an account of the geophysics of natural thermal activity.

Dr Wohlmann had a very uncomfortable time during the First World War, with the fanatical anti-German feeling that raged through the country. Although he was English, people thought his name sounded German. He retired from the official Balneologist's house to one on the outskirts of town and hidden by a high hedge, where some Rotorua locals imagined that the doctor kept in touch with Germany by radio. To make his situation less unpleasant, the Balneologist took his mother's maiden name, Herbert. Perhaps he is better remembered under that name for, as Herbert, he wrote his best-known book. During the war, Wohlmann treated hundreds of wounded New Zealand troops.

Wohlmann was replaced by John Campbell Duncan, whose first problem was a shortage of Rachel water in the Rotorua Bathhouse — an auxiliary supply had to be piped from a lake at Whakarewarewa — but whose major headache would be the maintenance nightmare of the Bathhouse interior.

References

1   T. E. Donne, Superintendent, to Minister of Tourist and Health Resorts, 22 August 1902. Tourist Department file 1901/5/10A.

2   A. S. Wohlmann to T. E. Donne, 3 October 1902, Tourist Department file 1901/5/10A.

3   A. S. Wohlmann to T. E. Donne, 11 December 1902. Tourist Department file 1901/5/10A.

4   Government Balneologist's report in Annual Report of the Department of Tourist and Health Resorts. *Appendices to the Journal of the House of Representatives*, 1902, H-2.

5   A. S. Wohlmann to Minister for Tourist and Health Resorts, 5 February 1903. Tourist and Health Resorts, 5 February 1903. Tourist Department file 1901/5.

6   A. S. Wohlmann to Superintendent, Department of Tourist and Health Resorts, 26 September 1902. Tourist Department file 1901/5.

7   Government Balneologist's report in Annual Report of the Department of Tourist and Health Resorts. *Appendices to the Journal of the House of Representatives*, 1906, H-2.

8   Dr I. C. Isdale. Queen Elizabeth Hospital Lecture to the Royal Society, Rotorua, 1980.

9   *The Dominion*, 12 January 1911.

10 *Rotorua Chronicle*, 6 January 1914.

6 A Maintenance Nightmare

Even before the Rotorua Bathhouse was opened in 1908 the white enamelled furniture began to turn black because the lead which had been used in the priming reacted with hydrogen sulphide in the moist atmosphere of the building. After its opening, the building was closed down while the furniture was repainted. All the junctions of the earthenware pipes leaked — in one case so severely that no water at all entered the building — and they had to be replaced by metal pipes. After a few months, however, even these looked like intestines with peptic ulcers.

This 1910 photograph of the rear of the Rotorua Bathhouse shows how it was built some 2 m above ground level, as indicated by the verandah. Except for the section at the right, which housed mudbaths, the basement contained only pipes and drains. There was no first-floor level at the dormer windows and there was an enormous amount of wasted space with the very high ceilings. *Alexander Turnbull Library.*

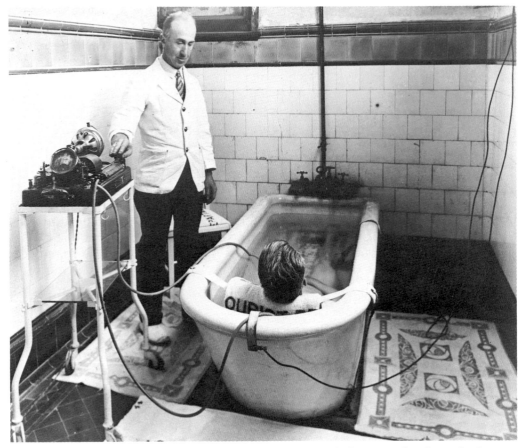

Like something out of a 1920s Fritz Lang film, this photograph illustrates the electric bath in use at the Rotorua Bathhouse from 1909 to about 1950. Constant overhauls were required for such equipment. *From Railways Department Album, Alexander Turnbull Library.*

Less than a year after the opening Lawrence Birks, Rotorua's Resident Agent for the Tourist Department, reported cracks in the concrete arches supporting the building, and at the end of 1909 the plaster had fallen from the ceiling in the men's hot vapour room. (The cracks in the concrete arches have enlarged slightly since 1909, but unlike Edgar Allan Poe's House of Usher, the Bathhouse is not likely to slip into a black tarn.)

During 1910 the wood-pulp plaster began to come away from the walls in several rooms; when it began to fall in large pieces from the ceiling, the department worried about injury to bathers. It was entirely the wrong material for a building filled with acidic steam; Bathhouse personnel sometimes had to change their clothes at midday because of the dampness. The problem was particularly bad during and after the 1920s. For some unknown reason the ventilating shafts and open rear basement were blocked in so that steam built up when the building was closed overnight. On some frosty mornings the doors had to be left open for several minutes before anyone could venture in. The situation became so serious that, in 1926, William Hill, the town's second Resident Agent, recommended that the building be pulled down and replaced. The demolition of a 17-year-old building that had, by then, cost £50,000, could have brought the Government down.

Apart from the 200 m² of plaster that needed replacement, parts of the ventilation turrets had perished and storm water came into the building. With the weight of the beams and the tiled roof, the walls were out of line in several places. In 1937, parts of the ceiling in the women's Priest's Bath area fell. Fortunately, no one was in the baths at the time. In this case it was not just plaster that fell, but timbers from a rotten temporary roof in the incomplete south transept of the building. The men's Priest Bath was put out of use because of the danger from falling plaster. In 1937 the main gable was more than 12 cm out of line at the plate.

There was disintegration in other buildings too. Dr Wohlmann reported as early as 1902 that part of the roof of the old Pavilion Baths had fallen. This original bathhouse was busiest from 1903 to 1908 when Aix massage was first introduced to Rotorua. During those years patients could have horizontal, Scotch, ascending, rain and needle douches. In 1905 Bradshaw's guide claimed that douches could in fact be recommended for such dissimilar complaints as hysteria, club foot, engorged liver and piles.[1] By the 1920s the Pavilion Bath building was impossible to repair because the roof would not support workmen. In 1926 an attendant narrowly escaped injury when a piece of timber crashed from the roof. The original bathhouse had become a poor shadow of the elegant spa that James Stewart had hoped for in his 1884 paper.[2]

When Sir Joseph Ward, who was mainly responsible for creating both the Tourist Department and the Rotorua Bathhouse, became Premier for a second time in 1929, plans were drawn up for 2 new Rotorua bathhouses to replace the Pavilion Bathhouse and the original Blue Baths. The plans were the work of J. T. Mair, the Public Works Architect, and the General Manager for the Tourist Department was delighted: "while the Reform party was in power not a penny was spent in new buildings, while the existing ones were allowed to reach the last stages of decrepitude. With the return to power of the Liberal party, the dawn of a new era is at hand. 'The winter of the discontent' of the people of Rotorua has been made 'Glorious summer'."[3] It was, however, to be the last summer for the original spa concept in New Zealand. Even with these replacements there were changes in approach. Instead of segregated nude bathing, the new Blue Baths were designed for integrated costumed bathing. They were also designed for swimming; one does not swim at a European spa.

The introduction of costumed bathing at Rotorua was an interesting follow-on to a meeting that took place 30 years earlier. When the new Tourist Department was about to take over the baths in 1901, it announced that new regulations to be brought in would ensure that all bathers wore the then respectable neck-to-knee costumes. At an angry public meeting held in Rotorua on 9 January 1901 people threatened to leave the district if the new rules remained in force after the meeting's feeling had been conveyed to the Hon. J. Ward. Bathers feared that the

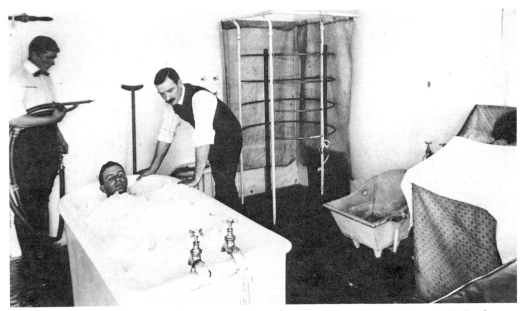

The temporary massage unit established behind the Duchess Bath from 1903 to 1908. In the corner is a needle douche and at right are a Turkish bath and a massage couch. It is a puzzle why the planners of the Bathhouse did not take notice of the success of this building in resisting acidic fumes — the walls here were covered by glass where there was acidic steam. *From Railways Department Album, Alexander Turnbull Library.*

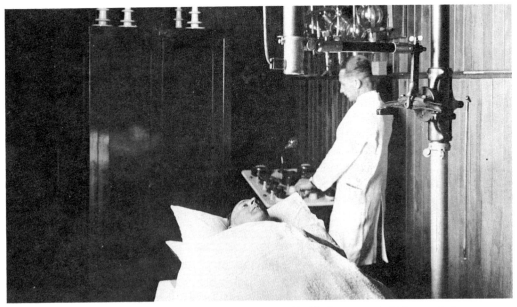

The Roentgen or x-ray at the Rotorua Bathhouse c. 1927. Hydrogen sulphide created maintenance problems with all the electrical equipment at the spa. *From Railways Department Album, Alexander Turnbull Library.*

The Ward Baths photographed in about 1935. The columns suggest Roman baths. *Rotorua Museum.*

wearing of costumes would allow those suffering from skin diseases to hide their condition. The Minister bowed to public opinion.

By the 1920s, however, those with psoriasis and other skin ailments were receiving alternative treatments and, as the public interest in hot spring waters gradually became recreational rather than medicinal, it became necessary to provide areas for family bathing — and costumed bathing returned. The Blue Bath became enormously popular.

The Ward Baths which replaced the demolished Pavilion Baths contained private and public Rachel pools and enclosed Priest pools, some of which came to be known as the Radium Baths. The Priest Baths were extraordinarily difficult to build. Very powerful pumps could not empty the springs and so work had to be done under water. Construction workers collapsed and fainted because of the concentration of hydrogen sulphide and the work could only be done on fine days, with a high atmospheric pressure and a northerly wind. All fittings had to be chrome plated and heart rimu was the only timber which lasted any length of time in the acidic water. Eight coats of paint were needed to get a reasonable finish in the Priest Bathrooms. The Ward Baths, which cost £45,000, were in use by 1931. The $40,000 Blue Baths were opened in two stages: the juvenile pool in 1931 and the main pool in 1933. The swimming pools were lit with arc lamps, a unique feature at the time. With a lounge on the ground floor and tearooms on the first floor, Roman columns around the baths and an Art Deco facade, the Blue Baths building was an attractive addition to the Rotorua spa.

References

1   *Bradshaw's Guide and Travellers' Companion for Wellington, Taranaki and Rotorua*, Wellington, Mills, 1905.

2   Stewart, James. *On the Establishment of a Grand Hotel and Sanatorium in the Rotorua District*, Auckland, Wilson & Horton, 1884.

3   B. M. Wilson, General Manager, to Minister for Department of Tourist and Health Resorts, 30 May 1929. Tourist Department file 24/43.

7 Transfer

Many people found it strange that a tourist department should administer medical facilities. The first step in changing this unusual situation was taken at Hanmer where the thermal pool area came under the control of the Health Department in 1921. At the same time, the future control of Rotorua was considered. At Hanmer, when the Health Department assumed control, the Sanatorium had been destroyed by fire so the Tourist Department only had to relinquish a few small bathhouses. In Rotorua, apart from the Sanatorium, and the £50,000 Bathhouse, the Tourist Department had been responsible for much of Rotorua's development, and it wasn't prepared to pass over what it had built up to another department.

There was, however, another aspect to the Rotorua situation. During the First World War a Services Convalescent Hospital had been built on Pukeroa, overlooking Ohinemutu. It became a problem when it was vacated by the Defence Department in 1921. As the empty hospital was intended to be used for orthopaedic medicine, it did not fit into the range of spa treatments administered by the Tourist Department. When, therefore, the Health Department took over the Pukeroa Hospital it meant that medical treatment in Rotorua was being carried out by 2 departments.

Although the Health Department felt that all treatments could be incorporated with the orthopaedic hospital, it was difficult to get the Priest's Bath waters up the hill to the hospital and it was a considerable distance to bring down patients to the Bathhouse. There was, therefore, some duplication of resources. Geothermal baths were part of the treatment of poliomyelitis cases at the Pukeroa Hospital. The water was pumped uphill, from the adjacent Kuirau lake a much shorter distance than from the Priest's Bath.

The directors of the 2 institutions, Dr W. S. Wallis, Superintendent of the Hospital, and John Campbell Duncan, the Balneologist, were considerable artists. They were also close friends and it must have been a difficult time for them. In 1929 Sir Joseph Ward considered closing the hospital and having it rebuilt in the Government Gardens, as part of the Tourist Department.

In the 1920s the Health Department had been keen to take over all medical functions in Rotorua, but the Tourist Department was determined to retain administrative control. In the 1930s, on the other hand, the Tourist Department was willing to hand over control of the Bathhouse, and the Health Department wanted to wait until that building was replaced. It was undoubtedly the maintenance nightmare of that structure that changed attitudes and policies.

Taken from a pavilion housing a camera obscura, this 1910 photograph includes the 1885 Blue Bath building at left, the 1890 Sanatorium with its onion-topped vents and in the rear, at left, the Balneologist's house. *Alexander Turnbull Library.*

Dr Duncan was sent to Europe to see what was being done in British, German and Czechoslovakian spas. The latest developments were to be incorporated in a building, or buildings, to replace the Rotorua Bathhouse and the Sanatorium. The latter would be replaced first.

Although the Sanatorium had never had to cope with problems caused by the condensation of acidic steam, because it had been designed in 1890, the building had become progressively less suitable for twentieth-century conditions. It was never large enough and almost always had a waiting list of patients. The institution had been designed primarily for those who could not afford to stay in hotels and Dr Wohlmann had suggested that, if his proposed hydro were built for paying patients, the Sanatorium "should be used for indigents".[1]

Diet, too, was an early problem; gout patients especially require a careful diet, and the Balneologist had noted that "fresh fruit, fresh vegetables, fresh fish are luxuries in Rotorua, and although I give to everyone of my patients a diet list suitable for his complaint, I know full well in my heart that this is more or less a farce".[2] There was very little farming or large-scale gardening on the Volcanic Plateau until the 1920s; immediately around Rotorua there were only 3 farms of consequence in the 1890s, on which the small town depended for butter, milk and fresh meat. There was no nearby supply of fruit and vegetables. So apart from bread, gouty patients could only rely on an ample supply of protein, the very type of food they should be careful of. Most of Rotorua's accommodation houses probably had menus which did not extend much beyond milk, potato, bread and mutton. Fruit was greatly treasured on the Plateau and for this reason

43

a kitchen garden had been established at the Sanatorium. It was the beginning of Rotorua's Government Gardens nursery.

Although a wing and a nurses' home had been added to the Sanatorium in 1908 and 1912 respectively, Dr Wohlmann had considered that the social side of the institution had remained at a standstill. The sitting rooms, particularly on the men's side, were, he said, "depressingly poorly furnished and dingy".[3] Dr Duncan, the second Balneologist, added that, while the staff did magnificent work, the building was unsuitable, "especially . . . for the better class of patient, who naturally objects to the lack of privacy in open wards and cubicles".[4] Duncan condemned the piecemeal construction of the place: "It has evolved, during the past fifty years, in a series of additions until now it is probably the most grotesque collection of bits and pieces it would be possible to find."[5]

The patients found the distance between the Sanatorium and the Bathhouse a greater drawback than the draughty verandahs on which they had to sleep when wards were full. In 1938 a patient commented sadly on the journey to and from the Bathhouse: "I wonder why no one thought that it might rain there sometimes and that patients . . . might get wet in transit. . . Patients who have to be wheeled to and from the 'San' to the bath house [about 300 m] . . . get the full benefit of the rain".[6]

The new building was to have 100 beds, arranged in wards of 1, 4 and 8, which were not to be specially separated into male and female sections. There was to be a communal room for lectures and music. The concept was similar in some ways to Dr Wohlmann's hydro, but it is doubtful whether the Labour Government, in planning the new Sanatorium, was very concerned about wealthy foreign invalids.

In 1939 £20,000 was spent on constructing a large raft foundation near the Rotorua Bathhouse. This type of foundation spread weight evenly over ground that could not be excavated. The war meant work on the building had to stop and only the foundations remain as a mystery object for tourists, who wonder at the purpose of such a massive construction.

Dr Duncan, who had been transferred to the Health Department, died in 1942. His successor, Dr A. J. M. Blair, had a different attitude towards balneology from that of his predecessors. Dr Duncan had been the last advocate of the spa principle, as against present day hydrotherapy, which is used as an adjunct to physiotherapy. Although he had pressed for the latest equipment and knowledge, he had laid considerably more importance on results obtained by water and mud alone. "In some of the cases undergoing mud-bath treatment," he claimed, "the effect has been almost miraculous . . . cases which have resisted all forms of drug treatment have cleared up in an almost magical manner".[7]

The transfer to the Health Department took place in 1947 and the Sanatorium was promptly closed. The building survived for another 25 years as a home for elderly men, but now the former nurses' home is all that remains of one of the only 2 spa sanatoria ever built in New Zealand.

Dr Blair, the third Balneologist, saw spa treatment as being complementary to clinical work done in hospitals. By the end of the 1940s a new attitude to the

The second Rotorua Sanatorium 1890–1949. *Photograph by Sidney Vaile, Auckland Institute and Museum.*

medical use of geothermal waters was evident. Rotorua's Queen Elizabeth Hospital was developed from the Second World War Services Convalescent Hospital and ever since has been the national hospital for the treatment of rheumatic diseases and other disfunctions of the locomotor system, such as cerebral palsy. Appropriately, its first Medical Superintendent was Dr Wallis, formerly of the Pukeroa Hospital.

In 1949 the Health Department's annual report contained the single most important statement in 150 years of written comment on New Zealand's medicinal hot springs. The author was the Director of Rotorua's new Division of Physical Medicine, Dr G. A. Q. Lennane:

> The old fashioned spa conception — a conception of treatment which has been responsible for the delayed knowledge of the treatment and causes of the rheumatic diseases — had to be abandoned, and the further exploitation of the mineral waters of Rotorua as miraculous cure-alls could not be condoned by the Health Department. A more rational and scientific outlook required to be developed.[8]

This new attitude affected not only Rotorua, but every area of hot springs used for bathing in the country. As a result, apart from the work that is carried out in the Queen Elizabeth Hospital in Rotorua, New Zealand's geothermal waters are now used almost exclusively for recreational rather than medicinal purposes. Where Waiwera was once a place to recuperate, it is now a place for a swim, a party or a barbecue. Where Parakai once had a massage department, it now has water chutes and large swimming pools.

References

1   Annual Report of the Department of Tourist and Health Resorts. *Appendices to the Journal of the House of Representatives*, 1902, H-2.

2   Report of the Government Balneologist in Annual Report of the Department of Tourist and Health Resorts. *Appendices to the Journal of the House of Representatives*, 1903, H-2.

3   Report of the Government Balneologist in Annual Report of the Department of Tourist and Health Resorts. *Appendices to the Journal of the House of Representatives*, 1914, H-2.

4   Report of the Government Balneologist . . . 1925 H-2.

5   Dr J. D. C. Duncan, Government Balneologist, to Director-General of Health, 14 July 1937. Copy in Tourist Department file 24/28.

6   Report of a letter from H. G. Heath, Palmerston North, recorded as "an inmate of the Sanatorium at Rotorua", to the Minister for Tourist and Health Resorts. The report is dated 25 February 1938. Tourist Department file 24/28.

7   Duncan, Dr J. D. C. "Rotorua Spa" in *New Zealand Official Yearbook 1940*.

8   Dr G. A. Q. Lennane, Director of Physical Medicine in Annual Report of the Department of Health. *Appendices to the Journal of the House of Representatives*, 1949, H-31.

8 The End of the Dream

By the late 1940s things at the Bathhouse were in a desperate state. A *Rotorua Post* article written in September 1948 claimed that the holes in the roof of the Bathhouse were so bad that the guttering had to be on the inside to catch the downpour when it rained.[1] In the same year it was suggested that the Bathhouse be turned into a museum of the Arawa people, a plan that to some extent eventuated in 1986 when an Arawa Hall was created in the south transept of the building.

The problems worsened. In December 1954 the *Post* described the working conditions and appearance of the place: "Down in the basement of the spa which is supposed to be world-famous, the mud-bath attendant worked in what looked somewhat less inviting than a concrete mixer . . . bare concrete, corroded pipes and sodden duckboards, lit by tiny, dingy windows, seemed to promise health more by black art than by natural means".[2] As an American visitor said in 1960, it was "enough to make sick people ill".[3]

In one of the many meetings held to discuss the fate of the Bathhouse, Mr Dan Kingi, representing the Ngati Whakaue people of Ohinemutu, urged the Government to retain the Bathhouse for its original function. He believed this would keep faith with the elders who had made a gift of the area, now occupied by the Government Gardens, for health and recreation purposes.

In 1963 the Rotorua City Council took over control of the Bathhouse, with £60,000 of Government money to convert the building for other communal purposes. It was still used for some bath treatments until 1966, when a hydrotherapy wing was opened at the Queen Elizabeth Hospital.

Many people still remember treatments in the Bathhouse. The popular physiotherapist, Arthur White, who worked in the building for 42 years, gave between 3 000 and 4 000 treatments a year. Some of his patients were very well known; Sir Bernard Freyberg and Sir Robert Stout (twice Premier of New Zealand) were among them. During the 1940s the Bathhouse gave an average of 30,000 baths and 25,000 massages and the building is still visited by people who were patients there from the 1920s through to its last year of treatment.

Mrs Alice Robinson, who was a bath attendant during the Second World War, described the atmosphere in the building. The bath attendants signed on at 8 a.m. and did not finish until 6 p.m. They had a 2-hour lunch break.

In cold weather our favourite meeting place [during the 2-hour break] was the Honeymoon Bath, so-called because couples could go there together. This bath . . . was less than the circumference of [present day] swirlpools, though many times the depth, like

47

The Postmaster Baths contained the most acidic bathing waters in New Zealand (apart from a natural pool at Taheke near Rotoiti). Fed by a spring called Waikirihou, the baths were opened in 1895. Bathers had to be supervised because of the amount of hydrogen sulphide discharged from the spring. The baths were covered over in 1952 because of deaths from the gas. *Alexander Turnbull Library.*

Rotorua in 1970, showing the art deco interior of the Ward Baths. *Photograph by Alan Warren, Rotorua Museum.*

a deep well. One had to walk down stairs to reach the bottom, then one sat on a circular seat. This left one's head just above water . . . Another favourite pastime was, after a bath of any kind, to wrap up in a hot sheet-sized towel and drape ourselves around the huge resting-room. This room had red plush window seats that went in a wide, circular sweep around the room — the height of luxury it seemed to us! For some reason we never ventured into the Russian Room — a huge dark, hissing room of steam. As I recall no patients ever had treatment there either.[4]

Mrs Robinson has many other amusing memories of the old Bathhouse, among them the vibratory chair used in treating overweight patients. The person was strapped in at the waist, wrists and ankles and, when the motor was switched on, was subjected to rapid, violent movements. Mrs Robinson particularly recalls the treatment of a large woman with pendulous breasts; when the motor began, the woman's breasts flipped over her shoulders, one after the other, faster and faster, with slapping sounds. It was very difficult for the attending staff to keep straight faces.

Of the other buildings in the Government Gardens, the original Blue Bath had been demolished at the end of 1932, while the second Blue Bath was last used for swimming in May 1982. The Postmaster Bath, south of the Government Gardens, in the Sanatorium Reserve, was closed in 1950 and, after several deaths, the spring was bulldozed in, during 1952.

All that remains of the various bathing facilities is the building that opened as the Ward Baths in 1931. A £23,000 Aix massage wing was added in 1965, intended as the first stage of a £140,000 plan to create a modern international spa. The cost over the next 4 years changed the Government's attitude, and in 1971, against some protests, the baths were let to Mr Neville Lobb.

After considerable alterations, the building reopened as Polynesian Pools in 1972. It was enlarged and altered again in 1985, and the complex now offers 2 large pools, 26 private pools, Priest and Radium Baths and Aix massage. Although some people bathe in the Priest Baths to treat rheumatic conditions, the pools are mostly used for recreation. A group of former European refugees living in Australia still, however, visit the Priest Baths every year for "the cure".

Attitudes and situations may simply have changed with time, but if Sir Joseph Ward and Thomas E. Donne could visit Rotorua today what they saw would not seem the fulfilment of the dream they had of Rotorua as the great spa of the South Seas.

References

1   *Rotorua Post*, 17 September 1948.
2   *Rotorua Post*, 7 December 1954.
3   *Evening Post*, 11 January 1960.
4   Alice Robinson, former bath attendant, Rotorua Baths. Typescript in Rotorua Museum archives.

9 Te Aroha — The North Island Rival

Waiwera was the first spa in New Zealand, Rotorua was, for several reasons, considerably the most important, but Te Aroha was the first geothermal water area to receive many thousands of bathers annually. It was, for several years, ahead of Rotorua.

As with Hanmer, Te Aroha's setting was almost as important as its water resources. The springs emerged from the side of Mount Te Aroha, the highest peak in the district. The Waihou River flowed at the foot of the mountain and the sheltered slope in between was ideal for growing trees and for laying out a town. There was native forest nearby and the scarp face of the Kaimai Range contrasted remarkably with the flatness of the Thames or Piako Valley lowlands.

Unlike Hanmer, Te Aroha has retained its spa appearance. Of all New Zealand's geothermal areas, the Domain at Te Aroha looks most as it did in Edwardian times. Some of the old bathhouse buildings remain and the formal gardens have been only slightly altered; they are not dotted with barbecue grills, and hydroslides don't loop their way downhill.

Before Te Aroha was developed, the local Marutuahu people valued the springs highly. As the hot water was salty, they believed it came from the sea, through a tunnel in the mountain. When he visited the area, Sir George Grey was led to the springs in 1849.

The original bath was made in the early 1880s after gold was discovered in the adjacent Waiorongomai Valley in 1881 and after the Hot Springs Hotel was built in 1882. (This first bath was a zinc-lined packing case sunk into the depression of a spring.) Gold was responsible for the immediate introduction of a coach service, which in turn helped develop a settlement that became a town district in 1887 and a borough in 1898. The arrival of the railway had a great deal to do with this expansion. For the first time in New Zealand it was easy for travellers to get to a hot springs area. After March 1886 visitors could travel by train from the centre of Auckland to within a few hundred metres of hot springs.

Before the railway reached Te Aroha work had begun in the springs area. A reserve of 8 ha had been gazetted in December 1882 and the construction of bathhouses began the following year.[1] An 1884 Government vote of £200 meant that a women's bathhouse could be completed so that when the Te Aroha Hot Springs Domain Board was formed that same year there were 3 bathhouses on

Te Aroha, photographed about 1890. The original ticket office is at the centre. Above it are the Octagon Pumphouse, the original No. 1 bathhouse and the original No. 4 bathhouse.
Alexander Turnbull Library.

the reserve. Fencing and tree planting began, and J. A. Pond analysed the water of 3 springs in February 1885. All contained a considerable proportion of sodium bicarbonate.

From 1885 Te Aroha was advertised in newspaper articles and tourist literature — it appeared, for example, in the Union Steamship Company's *Tourist Vade Mecum* — and this quickly brought an increase in the number of visitors. Travellers could reach Te Aroha directly by rail, whereas Rotorua was a 64 km coach journey from Tirau, and the difference showed up in the number of baths taken at each spa. From January to May 1886 18 686 baths were taken at Te Aroha, but Rotorua's total was only 5 314 for the 9 months from October 1885 to June 1886. Even before the railway, however, Te Aroha was ahead. Not only was it much closer to Auckland but the journey to it could be made by boat; the small vessel *Kotuku* steamed up the Waihou River from Thames. It was much more comfortable than travelling the coach roads to Rotorua.

An early problem facing the Domain Board was people using soap in the baths. Women were suspected of being the main offenders and the *Te Aroha & Ohinemuri News* recorded on 20 November 1886 that a caretaker had been detailed to keep a close eye on the use of soap. From the same paper it is interesting to learn the cost of developments 100 years ago. An attractive little building over the main drinking fountain cost only £75 to construct over the summer of 1886–87.

There were 7 bathhouses at Te Aroha by 1886, and they received considerable praise. Letters to the *Te Aroha & Ohinemuri News* in September 1886 expressed gratitude for the developments that had been carried out within the space of 3 years. A Mr J. W. Balfour, for example, was suffering from rheumatism in the

A rustic pumphouse built around the No. 15 spring. There were 22 springs in the Domain, some of which no longer exist. The No. 15 spring supplied hot water with a large sodium bicarbonate content. *Alexander Turnbull Library.*

head and feet when he arrived at Te Aroha, but after a 2 week bathing course he was no longer plagued by "uneasiness" in his feet. Another enthusiast was full of wonder that "the Domain Board have, with the small amount of money at their command, been able to erect six comfortable bath houses, and a tasteful drinking fountain, to say nothing of the fencing, extensive drainage and plantations . . . Wherever I go I shall, in the interests of humanity, make known the special virtues of the Te Aroha springs".[2]

The reputation of the Te Aroha waters gave local residents the confidence to forward a petition to the Minister of Lands, John Ballance, requesting a resident medical officer. Proper supervision of invalids' bathing was necessary. There had already been one death "which it is believed was accelerated by the use of one of the hotter baths"[3] and the petitioners were afraid that there could be other such cases. They offered to pay £150 a year towards keeping a doctor in their small area but there is no evidence that they ever did fulfil this offer.

With a Government subsidy of £50 per year, however, Te Aroha obtained the services of Dr Alfred Wright. He described himself as physician to the Thermal Springs Domain and in 1887 published a guide for invalids and visitors. Since he was also the author of *Digestion, the Passport to Health*, he was very enthusiastic about Te Aroha's sodium bicarbonate springs. It is difficult to resist the mental picture of trainloads of dyspeptics climbing the Domain to the No. 8 and No. 15 springs of drinking water and burping their way downhill to the railway station.

The Hot Springs Hotel, a symbol of Te Aroha's supremacy in 1885. It was to be answered by the Grand Hotel in Rotorua (1895) and Hanmer's Lodge (1898). *National Museum.*

Dr Wright was not exaggerating when he said that not many places had achieved fame in the short space of Te Aroha's few years of development. It was also true in 1887 that "Its fame as a watering-place has now quite eclipsed all others, including Rotorua." Wright considered that his spa offered serenity and repose: "there are no subterranean rumblings, tremblings, and other volcanic disturbances of a more or less appalling character, such as are perpetually taking place at Rotorua, and which render that place quite unsuitable as a resort for nervous invalids."[4] Dr Wright was, of course, alluding to the 1886 eruption near Rotorua, which briefly affected traffic to that spa.

Te Aroha's 7 bathhouses had various functions. One was reserved for women, 2 with shallow baths were generally used by children, 1 contained 8 private baths, and there was, as Dr Wright explained, "a bath-house a distance from the rest which is set apart for the sole use of natives".[5] There were 2 springs of drinking water, 1 of which relaxed, while the other confined, the bowels.

Many visiting the spa travelled on the steamships *Rotomahana* and *Enterprise*, through the sheltered waters of the Firth of Thames, as the southern extremity of the Hauraki Gulf was then called. The river steamers from Thames berthed at Turua, Hikutaia and Paeroa, on their voyages up the Thames or Waihou River to Te Aroha.

Several comfortable hotels were built at Te Aroha during the 1880s. The Club Hotel (later the Grand), opposite the Domain, was famous for its long (19 × 3 m) balcony which gave an extensive view of the scarp wall of the Kaimai-Cape

Colville Range. The dances or concerts held on the balcony on summer evenings came the closest to recreating in New Zealand a European spa atmosphere. From the hotel's rear balcony guests could see the distant smoke of trains from Auckland. When not puffing on their cigars the gentlemen would often be downstairs in the billiard room while the women were frequently found upstairs in 1 of 3 sitting rooms containing "a first class piano".[6] Visitors were assured that there was plenty of water for the WC at the end of the passage — a 400 gallon tank, in fact.

The Hot Springs Hotel, too, had "a splendid piano"[7] and those gathered on its first-floor verandah could watch the small steamers plying the Waihou. The Palace Hotel was noted for its prize billiard room table, and even the Waverley Private Hotel boasted something never found in modern hotels — a reading room. (These, of course, have been replaced by television rooms.)

Outside these establishments there were various attractions for visitors, including walks along the river, through the Domain (containing the springs and baths) and, above it, to the Spur, with a view over the immediate countryside. For the more energetic the top of Mount Te Aroha was a challenge; from the summit climbers could see from the sea to the Waikato and from Auckland to Ruapehu.

Another walk took tourists to the gold workings in the Waiorongomai Valley, while picnics and gipsy parties were held in the ravines of the scarp slope running north and south of the town. Buggies and brakes took groups to Lake Waikare and the most adventurous walked over the divide to Katikati. For the more sedentary the public library and reading room (open 10 a.m. to 9 p.m.) stocked the leading Home and colonial newspapers and periodicals, while the public hall was the venue for soirées, theatrical performances and concerts. Te Aroha in 1887 outshone Rotorua as a social centre.

Te Aroha also had the advantage of pleasant-tasting mineral waters. Bottling and sales began in 1886 and 2 years later the Te Aroha Soda and Mineral Water Company exhibited the waters at the Melbourne Centennial Exhibition. The town was certainly doing its utmost at this stage to make the most of its spa potential. Unfortunately, when Dr Wright announced in 1887 that the Te Aroha Sanatorium Company was being floated to establish a sanatorium in the town, the scheme was unsuccessful and Dr Wright left the district.

It was important that the spa be developed as rapidly as possible. As Rotorua became better known, it affected the numbers of bathers at Te Aroha, although the latter stayed ahead into the early 1890s. It wasn't until the railway reached Rotorua at the end of 1894 that the Volcanic Plateau centre began to draw ahead. Only after 1902, however, with extensive advertising by the new Department of Tourist and Health Resorts, did Rotorua's spa revenue exceed Te Aroha's.

Because of the very limited finances of the Domain Board, the rate of development in Te Aroha slowed down, but 1 of the two 1894 improvements was an important element of a successful spa. A tiny ticket office was replaced by a library, reading room and waiting room. The other improvement was not a success. Without an engineer to oversee operations the base of the new concrete swimming bath cracked and so it had very limited use. Some of the other struct-

Te Aroha Domain in 1905. The people are gathered around the No. 15 spring which, 2 years later, had a pumphouse built over it. The No. 2 bathhouse is the only natural bath still in use at Te Aroha. The reservoir at the right was enlarged to become the still existing tepid baths. *Photograph by Muir and Moodie, National Museum.*

ures built by the Domain Board were criticised for their simplicity. The private bathhouse, for instance, had no ceiling and a visitor worried about "larrikins"[8] admiring women bathers from over the cubicle walls.

The largest single development of Te Aroha spa was carried out in 1897 and 1898. The bathhouse constructed during these years was probably the most attractive in the country until the Blue Baths were opened at Rotorua in 1933. (The main bathhouse at Rotorua is slightly grotesque, with its verandah and Gothic elements added to the Tudor style.) Named after the Member for Ohinemuri, Mines and Railways Minister A. J. Cadman, the new Te Aroha building was sited on a terrace above the entrance to the Domain. With 19 tiled private bathrooms containing porcelain baths, the Cadman Baths, opened in May 1898, provided an attractive atmosphere for 60 years. Without the problem of acidic waters, the building cost a small fraction of the upkeep of the Rotorua Bathhouse and was vastly more appealing than any bathhouse there until 1908 when the main Rotorua bath building was opened. Even the floral porcelain lavatory pans at the Cadman Baths seemed designed for ornamental rather than other functions.

The Lands Department, as overseer for the Domain Board, thought that Te Aroha did and should provide for "people in good circumstances and precisely the class of people who ought to be attracted and encouraged to come".[9] Wealthy

The pond in the foreground of the Te Aroha Domain was formed around the No. 17 spring and the No. 15 spring was in the pumphouse at the right. Within the rustic fence was a reservoir which later became the tepid swimming bath. The nearest building contained the hottest spring (the No. 2). Beyond the No. 6 bathhouse was the gardener's house and at the left were the No. 1 bathhouse and the Octagon Pumphouse. *Radcliffe Collection, Alexander Turnbull Library.*

tourists made a spa a financial success. The Cadman Baths meant an increase in bath fees for Te Aroha, from £769 in 1898 to £954 in 1899.

This extra money encouraged a gradual replacement of all but 1 of the original bathhouses. (The No. 5 was later demolished.) The most popular, the No. 6, was rebuilt and enlarged in 1899. The replacement, carried out over a period of 6 years, were designed so as to blend with the Cadman Baths, and the new No. 6 and No. 1 bathhouses in particular were handsome little buildings.

The Department of Tourist and Health Resorts took over control in September 1901, and the Domain Board ceased to exist at the beginning of 1903. Direct departmental control had an immediate result for Te Aroha: Dr Kenny, formerly of the Rotorua Sanatorium, was appointed Resident Medical Officer. Before his arrival in March 1903, the £50 Government subsidy was not enough to keep doctors in this small town.

After the women's bathhouse (the No. 1) and the children's bath (the No. 4) were rebuilt, the Resident Medical Officer became concerned at the condition of the No. 7 bathhouse. This, built over a spring of warm sulphurous water, had 2 rooms 1 of which provided a free bath for local Maori people, while the other was

This 1905 photograph of the Te Aroha Domain shows, from left, the croquet and bowls pavilion, the band rotunda, the Cadman Baths, the meteorological station, the washhouse (for towels), the No. 3 bathhouse and the No. 7 bathhouse. The No. 1 bathhouse can be seen on the hill. *Photograph by Muir and Moodie, National Museum.*

used, very infrequently, by people with skin complaints. As Dr Kenny pointed out, the baths set apart for skin diseases "should be made as comfortable and inviting as possible, instead of, as at present, as dingy and miserable a looking place as one could very well find".[10] If the bath were made more attractive, fewer people would attempt to hide their skin conditions in order to get into the more popular pools.

The Domain at Te Aroha was made more attractive, in the same way as Rotorua's Government Gardens. Tennis courts, bowling and croquet greens were provided, the Waikino Brass Band and others played in the rotunda and Chinese lanterns lit the walks on summer evenings. Te Aroha retained some advantages over Rotorua. There was a library at the Domain and hill walks up to the bush-covered spurs of the mountain. Dr Wohlmann, the Balneologist, considered the Te Aroha Domain spur, like Conical Hill at Hanmer, a suitable slope for Oertel treatment. (Oertel was a German who achieved some fame by suggesting that graduated hill climbing was good for heart problems.)

Although a smaller establishment, Te Aroha was allocated the same sized tea house as Rotorua and Hanmer. It was almost as though this style of tea house was standard Department of Tourist and Health Resorts issue; one could imagine a

Te Aroha's tea house opened in 1908. After a few years it became the home of the Tourist Department's Resident Agent. *Alexander Turnbull Library.*

head office inventory with the Te Aroha entry — "Tea house, regular issue, 1." The Te Aroha tea house was not, however, as successful as Rotorua's. Oertel would have been very disappointed to learn that some considered it failed because it was on a rise and people couldn't be bothered walking uphill to use it. The building closed in 1923, the same year which saw the demise of the No. 3 bathhouse. This had been the massage building since 1905, but had become "absolutely untenable on account of delapidation [*sic*] due to the borer".[11] Massage rooms were then built onto the rear of the Cadman Baths.

Te Aroha's great problem was lack of water. Not only was the hot water supply limited but there was also insufficient cold water. Apart from the fact that the cold swimming bath leaked many thousands of litres a week, and that hardly anyone wanted to swim in it, it sometimes couldn't be filled in the summer because of town water requirements. In 1924 someone suggested that the cold bath could be heated by water from a newly discovered spring. It was found, however, that it would take a fortnight to fill the bath and then it would be stone cold.

There were 22 springs in the Domain area, 15 of which were hot, but some of them were extremely small. As early as 1898 a unique method was used to try and supplement the natural supply. Instead of boring, a horizontal tunnel was driven 45 m into a spur and 2 new springs were caught. The idea was put forward of constructing an "inhalatorium" halfway along this tunnel — that is, a room where people could stand in the intense vapour of the tunnel. This inferno-like suggestion came to nothing; it could have been extremely dangerous and the tunnel was used merely to collect water.

Looking down on the Te Aroha Domain from the Octagon Pumphouse where the gentleman has filled his cup. The No. 1 bathhouse was rebuilt soon after this 1903 photograph was taken. Across the road is the Grand Hotel. *Alexander Turnbull Library*.

Two of the most useful springs to Te Aroha were Nos 8 and 15, the ones which provided water for bottling. The original lease with the Te Aroha Soda and Mineral Water Company was terminated and a new one signed with Hancock and Company, which sold bottles of the mineral water, a shilling a time, at its Grand Hotel in Rotorua. When Rotorua's bathhouse opened the water was sold, at a penny a cup, from a cubicle in the foyer. Hancock's bottles were advertised as the "autocrat of the dinner table", and a well-known advertisement from the 1904–24 period read "Don't forget your Te Aroha". For many years Innes and Co. was a rival firm, bottling Wai Aroha and Lemon and Te Aroha. A third firm offered other rivals to Lemon and Paeroa, and finally, during the Second World War, a fourth firm, C. A. Clarke of Rotorua, entered the market with Te Aroha water mixed with various flavourings. Bottled Te Aroha water is still available at the Domain baths.

The bathing waters had a more problematic history. After repeated entreaties for a warm water swimming pool, the Government rebuilt an 1897 open bath which had never been used because it leaked. The old pool was covered by a building similar in style to the small bathhouses. Because of the popularity of the mixed bathing available at nearby Matamata it was decided to have costumed mixed bathing at the Te Aroha pool, which was opened in November 1928. One of the few remaining structures of the original spa, this bath is still popular despite its limited size. To make sufficient water available, the No. 6 and the No. 4 bathhouses were closed. The latter was demolished in 1931; the No. 6

59

At the tennis courts in Te Aroha, about 1910. At the left are the Cadman Baths, with the No. 3 bathhouse and the cold swimming pool at the right. *Alexander Turnbull Library.*

survived until 1936 as a reserve when the swimming bath had to be repaired.

The attempt to provide more water continued for 20 years from 1936, when the first bore was sunk in this geothermal field. As well as increasing the flow, the bore provided a tourist attraction in the artificial Mokena Geyser. Few people watching the uncorked champagne bottle effect of the bore realise that they are standing on the site of the old No. 4 bathhouse.

A second bore failed to produce enough water for a full-sized swimming bath and the search was abandoned after a DSIR investigation in 1956.

The Cadman Baths were closed in 1961 and the seldom used 1894 cold swimming bath was filled in. The magnificent old Hot Springs Hotel closed in the same year, so 1961 was, to a great extent, the end of the Te Aroha Spa. One minor alteration, however, meant that more bathers used the Domain. In 1968 the women's No. 1 bathhouse became a general private bath, which could be booked by telephone. It became very popular.

By 1962 the Domain was costing the Tourist Department £26,000 per year. The Government gave up control of the area in 1978, at the same time granting $100,000 towards further development. The No. 1 bathhouse was demolished the following year and all that now remains of the spa is the No. 2 bathhouse, the small tepid swimming pool, the Mokena bore or artificial geyser and pumps at the No. 8 and No. 15 springs. Part of the Cadman Bathhouse is now a spa museum. To some extent, the Domain is a memorial to the idea of a great spa in the Southern Hemisphere. Rotorua may have been the Government's choice for New Zealand's main international resort, but at Te Aroha the flavour of Edwardian days is less affected by modern development. There are no elements of present day structure and materials to coat the plan of 1901 with the technology of 1981.

Apart from its natural disadvantage of a limited hot water supply, there was an invisible brake on Te Aroha's development. Until 1915 (when Hanmer was taken over by the Defence Department) Te Aroha was regarded by the Tourist Department as New Zealand's third spa, and after 1915 as the second most important. If private enterprise had developed Te Aroha in direct competition with Rotorua, despite the former's superb setting, the variety of attractions at Rotorua would undoubtedly have still gained it more visitors and bathers than its rival.

References

1   Most accounts of Te Aroha state that the original, and most important, 20 acres of the Domain were given to the nation by Morgan or Mokena, a chief living at Te Aroha. A letter from the Commissioner of Crown Lands, 6 April 1977, indicates that the 20 acres were part of 53 900 acres sold to the Government in August 1878 (Deed 1302). It must, however, be remembered that many Crown Lands records were destroyed by a fire in 1952.

2   Captain J. Fraser in *Te Aroha & Ohinemuri News*, 4 September 1886.

3   Te Aroha residents and visitors petition to the Minister of Lands, November 1886. Department of Lands and Survey file 86/3676.

4   Wright, Dr Alfred. *Te Aroha, New Zealand: a guide for invalids and visitors to the thermal springs and baths*, Te Aroha Hot Springs Domain Board, 1887.

5   *Ibid.*

6   *Ibid.*

7   *Ibid.*

8   Arthur Dillon Bell's remark in the Domain visitors' book, as recorded in a letter from the Secretary of the Te Aroha Domain to the Minister of Lands, 5 September 1892. Department of Lands and Survey file 13417.

9   Annual Report of the Department of Lands and Survey. *Appendices to the Journal of the House of Representatives*, 1899, C-1.

10   Report of the Resident Medical Officer, Te Aroha, in the Annual Report of the Department of Tourist and Health Resorts. *Appendices to the Journal of the House of Representatives*, 1904, H-2.

11   Government Balneologist to General Manager, Department of Tourist and Health Resorts, 7 May 1923. Tourist Department file 96/29.

10 Hanmer — The South Island Sanatorium

If Hanmer had been planned by a landscape designer, its scale and proportions could not have been improved. Surrounded by hills but with the expanse of the Hanmer Plain on one side to prevent any sense of claustrophobia, the town has a special atmosphere, secluded from the pressures of city life.

At 360 m above sea level, the area has a bracing climate and its distance from the ocean is, as a 1900 guide book put it, "a guarantee against moisture, the bane of so many climates".[1] The usual wind is the warm nor'-wester. The winter, however, is another matter; snow can lie on the ground for a week. In 1899 most of the macrocarpa windbreak around the Springs Reserve was killed by a frost and a 1903 letter from the Sanatorium Manager gives a good idea of winter conditions: "We had a week's frost varying from 16° to 20°, the thermometer standing as low as 12°F, whilst the country for miles around here is feet deep in snow, the average in the grounds here being 5"."[2] When the well-known Rotorua physiotherapist, Arthur White, was offered a permanent position at Hanmer after he had been temporarily transferred there, he refused. The winters reminded him of those in England — and he'd emigrated to get away from the cold.

Hanmer, nestling near the far end of its inland basin, must have seemed, in the 1890s, like an oasis to coach passengers who had travelled across the wide plains. But although the coach run to Hanmer from the nearest railway station must have been a deterrent to some invalids, for many visitors the 38 km from Culverden to Hanmer was in fact part of the spa's charm. They felt a long way from their usual lives in Christchurch and Dunedin. The actual distance was magnified by the time it took to make the journey, so that the person taking the rest cure could "completely detach his mind from his too engrossing avocation",[3] as a Railways officer put it in 1904. This was what a spa should be — a small, unstressful world.

The atmosphere of the place influenced the Government Balneologist when he completed a brochure for the Government in 1907:

> Hanmer is indeed 'far from the madding crowd' and a goodly proportion of the visitors adopt the motto Dolce far niente. ['it is sweet doing nothing']. The mild dissipations of a game of croquet, bowls, or tennis, or at most a stroll to the top of Conical Hill, serve to fill the time between bathing, drinking the waters, sleeping and eating . . . In the evening . . . the broad verandah of the tea-house invites to lazy contemplation, the pipe of peace, and early to bed the better to capture that exquisite indefinable essence of unsullied morning which rewards the early riser.[4]

HANMER

HOT
SPRINGS.

"THE SPA" (GOVERNMENT ACCOMMODATION-HOUSE),
HANMER HOT SPRINGS.

A Pleasant Holiday Place.

The sanatorium at Hanmer which, for a short time, was known as "the Spa". This photograph and artwork formed the cover of a 1900 brochure. *National Archives.*

A winter's day in Hanmer, c. 1914. At left is the original bathhouse, with the men's swimming pool at right. The ironwork fence beyond the family group surrounds the No. 5 spring. *Alexander Turnbull Library.*

This sounded more like the rest cure than coping with hydrogen sulphide at Rotorua.

Although the springs of Mani-Rauhea — the plain of the shining tussock — had been known to the Ngai-Tahu people for centuries, the springs were "discovered" in 1859 when William Jones wrote to the *Lyttelton Times* to describe some hot pools that he had found. He had seen "what seemed to him a remarkable fog, and upon leaving his track to examine it, he discovered some holes which were filled with water of a temperature varying from milk-warm to almost boiling."[5]

A reserve of 1072 ha around the springs was proclaimed by the Nelson Provincial Government in 1860. The Waiau Gorge bridge was constructed 4 years later to provide access from Canterbury, but as no development took place Nelson lost interest in this distant territory.

Dr James Hector of the Colonial Laboratory examined the Hanmer Springs in 1867 and Sir Julius von Haast of the Canterbury Museum in 1870. An accommodation house established 4 km from the springs in 1862 became the Jollies Pass Hotel and its manager built a dressing shed next to the main bathing pool in 1878.

When Von Haast made his second visit in 1881 he considered that the springs should be developed, either by the Government, or by a large company. He

The amphitheatre of the Hanmer Plains from the summit of Conical Hill, c. 1904. The Lodge is close to the lake, while the Sanatorium and bathhouses are within the shelter belt square, right of centre. *Canterbury Museum.*

suggested "some amount of money ought to be spent towards embellishing that now rather dreary and bleak spot. Being surrounded by picturesque mountains, a delightful villegiatura would thus be created."[6]

Von Haast had an interested reader in William Rolleston, Minister for Lands. In 1883 the Lands Department excavated the main bathing springs to create swimming pools, one of which was fenced against the winds and to add privacy. (Only 4 of the springs were of any consequence.) The first bathhouse was also built that year, to contain 4 baths, each 2.4 x 0.6 m. An area of 2 ha was enclosed around the springs, with a macrocarpa windbreak. In 1885 a second accommodation house was opened, at Jacks Pass. More baths were required and a second bathhouse, built in 1888, had 8 baths.

The first brochure to publicise the area, issued in 1890, tried to convince readers that the 22 stopping places on the 112 km rail journey from Christchurch to Culverden relieved the boredom of the trip. And there were, it explained, plenty of cattle and sheep to look at. (The St Helens Station near Hanmer carried 80,000 sheep.) There were also 22 fords on the 38 km coach journey from Culverden to the springs.

Accommodation was a problem in such a remote area. The Jollies Pass Hotel was 4 km from the springs, and the Jacks Pass Hotel was some 2 km away — too

This 1904 photograph shows the men's swimming pool, built around a natural spring. This became the women's swimming pool when a larger pool was made available for the men. In turn, the original women's pool was then used by girls. *Auckland Institute and Museum.*

far for bathers who were often invalids. The Government offered concessions in 1886 for a company to build a hotel close to the springs; for the first 21 years the lease of 58 ha was to have an annual rent of only £5. There was little response, and no accommodation house was built at the springs until 1897.

Gas collected from the springs was used to heat a waiting room added, along with 2 more baths, to the second bathhouse in 1893. This room also served as a reading room, providing, with its armchairs, books and newspapers, the first relaxation other than bathing. (This was 10 years before the Tourist Department listed the requirements of a spa.) In 1894 a women's swimming bath, known as the Marian Pool, was opened; a separate men's pool had been used since 1893. This development was followed by a bowling green and a tennis court. A pump was attached to a spring so that visitors could drink the mineral water, which varied only slightly in the 10 springs and was described as tasting rather like over-ripe eggs.

The development of Hanmer's limited resources included both a scientific approach and pathetic detail. Dr C. Little was appointed Visiting Medical Officer to the Hanmer Thermal Sanatorium in 1895, while the caretaker's report for the following year mentioned "the inhaling of steam from the waters has also been found to effect wonderful cures; for this purpose I have placed an earthenware pipe over a hole on the top of one of the hottest pools so that persons wishing to inhale have the full strength of the steam."[8] These proved extremely popular, although, because the pipes had no U bends, there were undesirable consequences when "people suffering from bronchial or other afflictions expectorate or allow saliva to flow on to and around these pipes. It is also said that one old lady . . . was sick and inadvertently polluted the pool."[9] She was, no doubt, overcome by the savour of over-ripe eggs.

The Hanmer Sanatorium, 1904. When it opened in 1898 there was only 1 public fireplace. From the end of 1908 there was a Resident Medical Officer. Fire destroyed the building in 1914. *Photograph by Muir and Moodie, National Museum.*

Eighteen ninety-seven was an important year for Hanmer. A massage room was opened in the older bathhouse early in the year, but much more important was the provision of accommodation close to the springs. For 10 years the Government had had no success in attracting private enterprise to build a hotel near the bathhouses, and so was forced to construct an accommodation house described as a Sanatorium. Before it could receive its first guests in December 1897, however, the owner of the Jollies Pass Hotel opened a hotel close to the springs, so these 2 buildings put an end to the situation where people had lived in tents at the springs for 12 to 15 shillings per week.

The new hotel, opened as The Lodge, provided the same sort of high-class accommodation as did the Hot Springs Hotel at Te Aroha or the Grand Hotel at Rotorua. It contained 2 suites of private rooms, consisting of sitting rooms with bedrooms attached, 17 other bedrooms, along with a drawing room, smoking room and dining room. Similarly, the Government Sanatorium offered a women's drawing room, a smoking room and a general sitting room.

For several years the Hanmer Sanatorium was a sanatorium in name only, being merely a lodging house where invalids could stay while they were taking the baths. It was intended for people who couldn't walk any distance. First-class accommodation was available for 40 shillings a week, second-class for 20 shillings. Most of the bedrooms were first class. This turned out to be an error as a large proportion of wealthy visitors preferred the greater comfort of the new Lodge. So many people required cheap accommodation in the summer months that in January 1898 the manager was instructed to erect tents for "second-class visitors" and within a few years additional second-class accommodation had to be added to the Sanatorium.

When Hanmer's original Lodge opened in 1897 it provided more comfort than the Government Sanatorium. There were bowls and croquet, and rowing was available on a small pond behind the hotel. *Auckland Institute and Museum.*

Another mistake was saving money on heating — "the house was very cold in the winter owing to there being so few fireplaces. The 1st class dining room has no fireplace . . . the smoking room is also much complained of during the winter months because it has no fireplace in it."[10]

Among the directions for the administration of the Sanatorium was the statement that "old and decrepit guests may have their meals in bed".[11] The manager was also instructed to retain the luggage of those who would not pay. He had to keep a produce and poultry book, a house book, a garden book, a furniture book, a stores account book, a monthly receipts and expenditure journal, and a record of the names of guests and the number of meals sold. Some of the guests were sent by the Patients' (Hospital and Lunatic Asylum) and Prisoners' Aid Society.

A gas holder was placed to collect the methane from the springs in 1898. This was used to light the Sanatorium. More improvements were provided, including a Vichy massage douche. In 1900 the gardener's wife got a washhouse in which to launder the bathhouse towels. She must have been delighted, after doing the washing in the open air for 15 years, with 11°C frosts.

A *Christchurch Press* reporter visiting at the turn of the century found "everything . . . looking in apple-pie order, thanks to the unremitting attention of Mr and Mrs Rogers [who managed the baths and the grounds]". The reporter also noted that the run to Hanmer was becoming popular with cyclists, "the only drawback being about a couple of miles of river bed, with several streams to wade".[12]

A third bathhouse added in 1900 contained 8 baths and a Turkish bath. The 2 ha of garden had been extended to 5 ha and the settlement looked less bleak on the otherwise treeless plain. A croquet lawn was laid down and there were

Hanmer in about 1904, showing, at left, the drinking pavilion; the box structure caught gas from the springs. Next to the gas holder is the women's swimming pool. *Alexander Turnbull Library.*

attractive walks through lawns and trees. The Lodge, providing something of the luxury of a European spa, was a comfortable resort for tourist and invalid.

On 1 April 1901 control of the Government facilities at Hanmer passed over to the Tourist Department. The enormous amount of development the department did at Rotorua wasn't necessary at Hanmer and Te Aroha, the third and second most important spas, because most of the facilities had been completed by 1901, when the Tourist Department was created.

The new controlling body did, however, make 2 changes in 1902. A massage building was opened and a masseur and masseuse were added to the staff. The other modification was not successful. Because the department sensed that the public believed the Hanmer Sanatorium was for the accommodation of invalids only, the name was changed to the Spa and it was advertised as a comfortable residence for all holiday guests. The *Christchurch Press*, in 1907, considered it was "unfair for the Government to compete with a first and second class boarding house",[13] and recommended that the place should be run as a proper sanatorium, with medical supervision.

Some of the department's improvements were popular, others were not. The broad verandah on a tea house similar to Rotorua's was much enjoyed. Opened in 1904, the tea house was run by "the Miss Pughs". The decision to provide a large cold water swimming bath was extraordinary. The idea was to keep purely recreational visitors away from Hanmer's limited hot water supply but, as happened with the cold water baths at Te Aroha, the pool was not a success. Opened in 1905, it only became popular when hot water was piped to it in 1912.

In place of the rustic pavilion where people coped with the flavour of well-ripened eggs, a tiled pump room was provided. This, the *Press* sourly claimed, "bore a strong resemblance to a butcher's shop".[14]

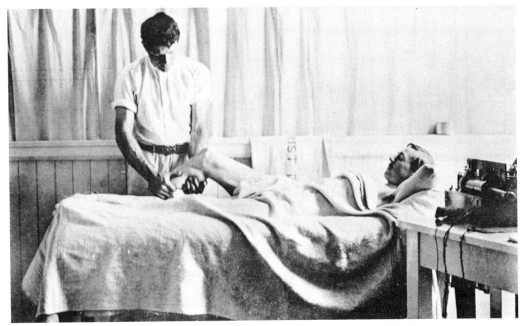

The Tourist Department established a massage section at Hanmer in 1902. Dry and electric massages were provided but water pressure was inadequate for effective Vichy or Aix massage. From J. and J. Dodds, *Hanmer Springs Illustrated*, c. 1910, C. A. McEvoy photographer.

The Tourist Department rethought its accommodation policy, phased out the "Spa" and reintroduced the "Sanatorium". This institution, a proper sanatorium, with a nursing staff, opened in December 1908, and by the following February had a Resident Medical Officer. The second Medical Officer, Dr J. D. C. Duncan, later became the Balneologist at Rotorua.

The major problem for a spa at Hanmer was an insufficient natural supply of hot water. An Auckland church minister was employed as a dowser to find more geothermal water and boring began in 1911. A successful probe near one of the natural springs provided hot water to heat the cold swimming bath. There was, however, a side issue to the bores at Hanmer. It is believed they altered the nature of the drinking water, which, when analysed, was found to contain a lot of borax. Notices were posted around the spa warning people not to drink more than 1 pint (600 ml) of the Hanmer mineral water a day. Any more than that amount caused stomach upsets.

By 1909 the Tourist Department was losing £1,500 a year on its Hanmer operations. In an attempt to get more people to the spa, the Works Department spent £9,000 on improvements to the Christchurch–Hanmer Road, and kinematograph views of the spa were shown at the Christchurch Industrial Exhibition in 1912.

The Sanatorium, which had accommodated 18 patients, was destroyed by fire the day after World War I began. Although work continued in a boarding house, View Brae, the war meant the end of Hanmer as a spa in the European sense.

Hanmer's tea house was of the same pattern as those at Rotorua and Te Aroha. When it opened in 1905 it was managed, according to Tourist Department records, by the "Miss Pughs". *Alexander Turnbull Library*.

After 1918 it continued to be a tourist resort and an important hospital centre, but the 2 functions were separated and the hospital was not primarily concerned with the use of geothermal water.

At the end of 1915 plans were drawn for a Defence Department Hospital capable of accommodating 200 men, most of them in 2 octagons similar to those of the Services Convalescent Hospital at Rotorua. The hospital, opened in June 1916, was the first of 3 separate blocks of the Queen Mary Hospital. The Surgeon-General reported to the Minister for Health in 1917:

> I am now confident that the climate and the surroundings [of Hanmer] are particularly suitable for shell-shock and neurasthenic cases. They certainly do better there than at Rotorua. We are therefore fortunate in having two specialised institutions — one at Hanmer for the cases already mentioned and another at Rotorua where the so-called curable incurables can be again made useful members of the community.[15]

In January 1921 the Queen Mary Hospital was handed over to the Department of Health. Dr Chisholm, who became Medical Superintendent, held that position for 23 years, dying the same year as his medical predecessor at Hanmer, J. D. C. Duncan. A separate women's block was opened in October 1926 and a new men's block late in 1940. The only real link between the hospital and the fact that Hanmer is a geothermal area was the use of shallow immersion baths as a secondary treatment in the extensive massage department. Patients in the 1920s and 1930s were very often suffering from hypertension and anxiety states, but joint disabilities were also treated.

The Health Department also took over the Tourist Department's activities at Hanmer, in December 1921, but the resort could not achieve the same sort of advertising under the new administration. A new bathhouse (for private baths) and massage block were, however, built in 1930, the same year that the 1883 and 1888 bathhouses were demolished. New bores were drilled in 1936 because of diminishing water pressure.

The 1926 publication *For a healthful holiday! Hanmer Springs* differed from the many brochures which had preceded it. In not evaluating the character of Hanmer's water and the extent of its bathing amenities, but concentrating on the scenic beauty of Hanmer's trees and mountains, the pamphlet echoed a change that was taking place in tourist literature throughout the country: holiday resorts were for everyone and they offered varied activities. By the 1920s the district boasted an attractive golfcourse, good fishing and, with improved roading, easier access to mountains and tramping routes. The springs were described merely as "an additional lure".

With the town becoming a general tourist centre, the Lodge was rebuilt as one of the most interesting hotels in New Zealand and the optimism about the area is clear when one remembers that this very large building was reconstructed in 1931 and opened in 1932, right in the heart of an economic depression. A 1933 jubilee book celebrating 50 years of development since the first Hanmer bathhouse indulged in purple prose and impressive terminology when describing the new hotel: "For the motorist there is a Porte Cochere, a necessary adjunct to the guest upon arriving, no matter the climatic conditions." Another passage describes a terrace as "a most adorable spot where the sunworshippers may gather in perfect bliss".[16]

While general facilities improved, however, the Hanmer Springs Progress League was concerned at the lack of development of the spa amenities. A 1934 League deputation claimed that "since the Health Department had taken over the bathing pools from the Tourist Department in 1921 . . . the facilities had been curtailed instead of being improved."[17] The general public, the League argued, could not have private baths because these were occupied by hospital patients. The deputation, turning envious eyes towards Rotorua's Blue Baths, considered that a similar pool for mixed bathing was needed at Hanmer.

From 1943 the Queen Mary Hospital was re-orientated to the treatment of functional nervous disease, which meant that the baths were no longer needed for the treatment of rheumatic conditions. Since the 1940s the hospital has also been involved in the detoxification of alcoholics. Outside the work of this institution, the history of Hanmer from 1933, when the Progressive League was formed, until 1978, when a complex of open air pools was opened, was one of frustration for local interests.

The principal bathing facilities until the late 1970s were 3 small swimming pools dating from between 1893 and 1908. Constant requests for improvements were turned down by Health and Tourist Departments alike and until the 1970s private interests were prevented from developing new facilities because of the thermal water needs of the hospital. As a result, the only alterations to the

Taken about 1904, this photograph shows, from left, the 1900 bathhouse, the 1888 bathhouse and the 1883 building. The last 2 bathhouses were demolished in 1930. *Auckland Institute and Museum.*

Hanmer baths from 1933 to 1978 were the introduction of mixed and clothed bathing and the closing of the private baths.

Hanmer was only a spa in the European sense from 1883 until 1915 when the Defence Department took over the geothermal resources. From 1916 on it was a specialised hospital area, with some recreational facilities. Only the bores which have been used to enlarge these facilities tell today's visitor that the complex of open air pools at Hanmer is any different from the public swimming centres to be found in most New Zealand towns and cities apart from the occasional sight of snow around the steaming baths.

References

1 *The Hanmer Hot Springs and How to Get There. A sanatorium for invalids and resort for the holidays*, Wellington, Government Printer, 1900.
2 J. B. Gould, manager, Hanmer Sanatorium, to Superintendent, Department of Tourist and Health Resorts, 22 July 1903.
3 Railway Officers' Institute, quarterly report, December 1904.
4 Wohlmann, A. S. *The Mineral Waters and the Health Resorts of New Zealand: Hanmer*, Wellington, Government Printer, 1904.
5 *Lyttelton Times*, 20 April 1859.
6 Haast, Julius von. 'Further notes on the thermal springs in the Hanmer plains, provincial district of Nelson' in *Transactions of the New Zealand Institute*, Vol. 14, 1881.
7 J. Rogers, caretaker, Hanmer Plains, Crown Lands report. *Appendices to the Journal of the House of Representatives* C-1, 1896.
8 J. Rogers, caretaker, to Superintendent, Department of Tourist and Health Resorts, 19 January 1903. Tourist Department file 1901/153/9.

9 A. Barron, Assistant Surveyor General, to D. McDonald, Manager, Sanatorium, 10 January 1898. Lands and Survey Department file 35108/130.

10 F. Stephenson Smith, District Surveyor, Kaikoura, to the Surveyor General, Wellington, 20 March 1900. Department of Lands and Survey file 21085/356.

11 "'Hansprings': the springs through the years" in Round, L. F. *Hanmer Springs Golden Jubilee 1883–1933.*

12 *Christchurch Press*, 8 October 1900.

13 *Christchurch Press*, 25 April 1907.

14 *Ibid.*

15 Memorandum for the Minister of Health regarding Surgeon-General Henderson's report on Hanmer, 13 October 1917. In Department of Public Health, Hospitals and Charitable Aid file 37/16.

16 Round, L. F. *op. cit.*

17 *Christchurch Times*, 6 December 1934.

11 Maruia Springs

No other major springs in New Zealand have been so affected by isolation as those at Maruia in the northern South Island. First discovered by Europeans in 1864, the springs had doubtless been used for centuries by the Ngai Tahu as they travelled the old greenstone trails of the area. Lying 64 km from Reefton, 80 km from Murchison and 56 km from Hanmer, the springs are far from any town or city, and inadequate roading meant that, generally, no car could reach Maruia before 1928, and then only from Reefton.

By the beginning of the twentieth century, various local bodies were asking for Government assistance with providing access to Maruia. Tourist Department officer Frank Moorhouse's inspection and report were the first of many. Journeying from Reefton in 1902, he noted that "a good road is made for fourteen miles,

The Lodge at Hanmer, one of New Zealand's most famous hotels. Its Spanish style was unusual in the early 1930s. *Photograph by W. A. Taylor, 1932, Canterbury Museum.*

Maruia Springs in 1951. The bathhouses had to be protected against floods by groynes of rock. *National Archives.*

then a rough pack track for fifteen miles through bush. We crossed several rivers, then four miles of grassy plain, then six miles up the Maruia River bed, crossing and re-crossing the river several times".[1]

Moorhouse and his companions found that the Inangahua County Council, based in Reefton, had done some work in the preceding 2 years. Earth had been cleared from a landslip covering the main spring, and a small reservoir for the hot water had been dug and lined with wooden slabs. There was a race from the reservoir to another hole for bathers, and a hut had been erected and forest cleared for horse paddocks.

A sample of spring water drew an unenthusiastic assessment from the Government Analyst — the main solid was soda, he said, with "traces of sulphates and chlorides".[2] The Tourist Department made no improvements.

To give those making the long journey a chance to rest, the Inangahua County Council built a halfway house. As the country chairman pointed out in 1903, had there been a proper road, many people would have been willing to erect a true accommodation house at the springs themselves. After all, as the *Reefton Herald* reported in 1904, the Surveyor-General himself said that the springs' curative properties were "admittedly superior to any . . . in the colony".[3]

After great difficulty in reaching the springs, because of floods, the District Surveyor reported that the area could be entered from Nelson (via the Matakitaki Valley) after 3 days' travel by horse and trap, at a cost of £5. Alternatively, it would take 10 hours to reach Maruia from Reefton. By this time the original bath had disappeared; the bath, he explained, "is obtained by scooping out a hollow in the sand and shingle at the end of the race. Every flood destroys the bath, but as there are picks, shovels and crowbars in the hut, there is not trouble making fresh ones."[4]

The surveyor was optimistic, too, about the future: "All residence sites will be on the south side of the river where there is a river flat well above flood level . . . and having a fine, sunny position, necessary for patients." He suggested fluming the hot water across the river. With a "great number of baths" and the "necessary comforts and conveniences for a health resort",[5] Maruia Springs could be a mecca for those seeking relief from various ailments. The waters, the surveyor claimed, had given relief to goldminers and coal miners suffering from rheumatism, sciatica and lumbago. As a drink, the water could greatly improve chronic indigestion and insomnia.

When the Murchison Branch of the Inland Communication League urged the Premier, Sir Richard Seddon, in July 1904, to open up the road to Maruia from Murchison and Reefton, "for the benefit of the large population on the West Coast and Nelson",[6] the Tourist Department informed Seddon that nothing had been done up till then because of the springs' inaccessibility. And when the Government Balneologist, based in Rotorua, was asked for an opinion, he replied that the water at Maruia had "no special advantages over the sulphuretted springs already in the possession of the Department".[7] Despite such lack of encouragement, however, a Government grant of £200 was eventually made for improvements to Maruia Springs and, using this money, the Inangahua County Council built wooden bathhouses in January 1905, and a suspension bridge across the stream.

Reporting on these changes, the *Nelson Colonist* gave a picture of the situation at the springs in March 1905. The main spring had been slabbed again. The bathhouse contained 2 large wooden baths which were filled by dipping the water from the pool alongside. But as the temperature of the spring water was 54.4°C, bathers would leave the water in the baths and, when a bath was required, would run off a quarter to a third of the water, filling it up with fresh spring water until a temperature of about 37.8°C was reached. After the bather had spent a little time in the bath, the article suggested, "more hot water can be added till 110 or 112 degrees [F] is reached, which is hot enough for comfort".[3] (Most present-day bathers find anything over 40°C too hot.)

Apart from the hard work involved, visitors must have been concerned about the lack of hygiene. The *Nelson Colonist* was reassuring on this point: "At night the baths were emptied and refilled, and early next morning it will be found that the heat is so far retained that not more than seven or eight buckets of fresh water are required to bring the temperature to the right thing." Although the paper admitted that this was a "rather primitive arrangement", it hastened to add that if several people were at the springs at one time, "after the first day, of three baths a day, there need not be any squeamishness". The article continued: "In taking the baths, it is usual to drink a moderate amount of the water from the pool after each bath."[9] Presumably this water was drawn from the spring reservoir, rather than the bathing tubs.

The *Nelson Colonist* writer made the useful suggestion that the route over the Lewis Pass to Canterbury be improved, as Maruia Springs was closer to Hanmer than to either Reefton or Murchison. Keeping Nelson interests in mind, however, the article suggested that the Maruia-Glenroy saddle was the cheapest route to open up the springs.

There was another dimension to Maruia's problems, as the *Kumara Times* pointed out. While "males had derived great relief from a course of bathing at Maruia Springs", women suffering from ailments were generally unable to take advantage of the waters "by reason of hardship and inconveniences entailed in travelling there".[10]

Although nothing was done to improve communications, accommodation was added, in the form of another hut put up by the Inangahua County Council during 1905. The new hut contained 3 rooms lined with linoleum and boasted 4 portable beds with spring mattresses. It was a considerable improvement on the council's 1902 hut, which slept only 2 people, in bunks, and on the original accommodation — a 3-roomed slab hut erected by a Mr Rosser at the turn of the century, to attract visitors to the springs.

In 1906 the Tourist Department sent an officer to report on the situation, but he was unable to get beyond Murchison. The lack of access created a vicious circle in the arguments against Government development. Here is the Superintendent of Tourist and Health Resorts writing in 1906: "Without a proper vehicle road invalids cannot be satisfactorily conveyed to Maruia . . . there is an entire absence of the comforts which are necessary in the case of invalids undergoing treatment for rheumatism and allied complaints".[11] It was a reversal of statements made by the department about some other hot springs areas, such as Te Puia and Morere; in those places, the department was most enthusiastic about improving communications.

The access problem was no better at the beginning of 1908 when the Christchurch *Press* recorded the experiences of a party making their way from Hanmer to Maruia Springs: "Of the track there were only traces met with here and there, but one of the party, by means of a compass, was successful in piloting the party to the desired goal . . . Some parts of the route were so steep that the travellers had to dismount and ascend like monkeys, by their hands and feet".[12] The pleasure of the journey was not increased by their having fly-blown blankets.

And Maruia Springs had yet another problem — the changing pattern of the river, over its shingle bed, constantly threatened the springs themselves, as well as the accommodation. Netting protection was set, for the first time, in 1908. In that year, too, the Tourist Department paid for the building of a small bathhouse for women.

During the First World War there was a suggestion from Reefton that a sanatorium be established at Maruia. Robert McNab, the Minister for Tourist and Health Resorts, did not agree, as he was already concerned about losses entailed in Government sanatoria at Rotorua and Hanmer. Another deputation, this time from the Inangahua County Council, pressed the Government in 1920 to complete the road from Reefton. Again, the road was not improved but work was carried out around the springs. A new women's bathhouse was constructed, with 5 concrete, rather than wooden, baths. A 1925 report was not, however, very complimentary about their appearance: they "look more like Egyptian tombs than anything else, and do not appear at all inviting".[13] The men's bathhouse could boast only 3 enamel baths.

By 1925 you could drive from Murchison to Springs Junction, 14 km from Maruia, but from there on, the Chief Clerk of the Tourist Department reported, "it is not advisable to take a car".[14] The isolation, though, was soon to be ended. The last stretch of road was being constructed and within a year, said the clerk confidently, people would be able to motor right through to the Maruia Hot Springs.

Later that year the Tourist Department's General Manager dashed any hopes for large-scale Government development at Maruia when he wrote to the Minister: "I do not consider that for a number of years to come they will be used by tourists, in the proper sense of the word."[15]

At last, in February 1928, the road from Reefton to Maruia Springs was completed, making it possible for cars to visit the springs in any weather. For some years before this a few drivers had managed to get through, but there was always the danger of being marooned if the weather changed. Professor Arnold Wall, travelling to the springs, preferred to walk some of the rough 10-mile section between Springs Junction and Maruia because he could not bear what he considered was cruelty to the cars. He claimed that he had not believed it was possible for cars to do what he saw done that day.

In this isolated situation conditions were primitive and control difficult. In 1928 a bather wrote to his MP to complain that deerstalkers had taken over the only good building and were leaving bones on the floor. Rheumatic sufferers were forced to camp out in tents and, with snow on the hill-tops and a south-easterly wind blowing, the writer was so cold he could hardly hold his pen.

The following year, 1929, the Government called for tenders to lease 40 ha of the Maruia Springs Reserve next to the springs, with the provision that the successful tenderer would erect an accommodation house to the satisfaction of the Minister for Tourist and Health Resorts. None of the tenders was, however, accepted and the Tourist Department decided in 1930, with work beginning on the Lewis Pass Road, to wait until the road was extended closer to the springs, in the hope this would increase the value of the lease.[16]

Tenders were called again in September 1930, to the indignation of the Misses Morris of Reefton, who had previously lodged the highest tender. In this second round they offered "One pound per annum more than the highest of any other tender that you may receive".[17] Renovations were made in the same year to the bathhouses and huts — with the exception of the original hut, which was condemned. (The 2-roomed hut was valued at £3.)

The men's bathhouse now had 6 enamel baths, 3 with stains and 3 without. There had been difficulties regarding lack of labelling for the bathhouses: "As there is no notice outside to distinguish one from the other, embarrassing situations sometimes arise," the *Otago Daily Times* reported.[18] The correspondent also claimed that a woman who had come to treat her rheumatism also cured her goitre.

The Morris sisters' tender was accepted after the second publication of notices. The terms included responsibility for the springs. They reported in March 1931 that they had found it necessary to appoint a bath attendant. By May they had had a site opposite the springs surveyed for the construction of an accommodation house. A considerable area of beech forest was cleared to allow for a foundation well above flood level.

By January 1932, the *Westport News* could report that the construction of a hotel at Maruia Springs was well advanced.[19] Designed by a Mrs Ainder, the building was unusual in that its back faced the then incomplete Lewis Pass Road, with a drive that curved around to a broad portico. The design's many attractive features included a heavy beamed ceiling in the sitting room, and large windows looking out to the Maruia River and Springs. The accommodation house was built of local native beech timber and the fireplaces were of local stone. There was one extraordinary drawback — the bedrooms could only be reached by an outside staircase.

The fact that by 1932 there was a charge for the use of the baths drew some criticism but, as the General Manager of the Tourist Department pointed out, the Morris sisters were entitled to a return on the money they had spent on the Chateau, and on the caretaker. In any case, one male and one female bath were reserved free of charge "for such persons who are certified as indigent".[20]

The Nelson Progress League reported in May 1932 that there were 27 km of road to complete over the Lewis Pass, a road that would make the Springs accessible to the people of Christchurch. As there was no guarantee at that stage that the road *would* be completed within a few years, it was a brave venture, on the part of the Morris sisters, to build a 60-room hotel. They worked towards finishing half of it by the spring of 1932.

The road had not been completed by 1934 and work stopped on the hotel, after the Misses Morris had invested £8,600 in the project. The lack of traffic meant that, for several years, the Chateau remained incomplete, with one end blocked off by corrugated iron.

The road from Murchison was finished in 1936 and the Lewis Pass Road in 1938, but difficulties at the springs did not end. In 1939 a heavy snowfall caused the roof of the men's bathhouse to collapse on the morning of 28 July. Luckily, no one was hurt.

During the war the Morris sisters offered the Chateau for use as a hostel. By this stage the bathhouses were falling to pieces and the men's baths had lost most

The Chateau Maruia Springs, c. 1934. Timber for the hotel, which replaced a collection of small accommodation huts, was cut from the surrounding beech forest. Fire destroyed this unusual building in 1968. *National Archives.*

of their porcelain. The water still had to be drawn by bucket. In 1941, however, both bathhouses were rebuilt.

The Hon. Robert Semple, renowned for his vivid descriptions, was typically forthright when interviewing a deputation that called for the Government to take direct control of the baths in 1943: "I've had dips there. The last time I think there were three or four dead rats in the pool".[21] (From a later newspaper account it appeared that he was in fact referring to the springs' reservoir rather than the baths.) Mr J. K. McAlpine MP capped the comment in 1952:

> I have never seen anything more dilapidated or disgustingly filthy and uninviting than the Maruia Hot Springs at present . . . the water is as black as strong billy tea . . . the only means of utilising it is by the primitive method of dipping a kerosene tin into the black hole of Calcutta and tipping it into an ordinary household bath . . . on a cracked concrete floor surrounded by an utterly dilapidated wood and corrugated iron shack.[22]

McAlpine did not take into account the fact that for years the Morris sisters had been attempting to get Government assistance to build new baths on the same side of the river as the hotel, and to have a road constructed from the Lewis Pass Road around to the front of the hotel and to the bridge which led to the bathhouses. Nor did he mention that the owners had created terracing for the intended new baths, or that they had installed hydro-electric works to light both the hotel and the bathhouses.

McAlpine's letter was, though, an attempt to get something done and his strong words seem to have helped draw the area to the Government's attention. They set aside £500 in 1952 for preliminary work at the springs.

Access via the Lewis Pass Road meant a revival of interest in the Maruia Springs. They were, some felt, ideal to be a second tourist resort in the northern

This 1951 photograph shows the interior of the Maruia Springs bathhouse. There were concrete baths for women. *National Archives.*

South Island, second, that is, to Hanmer. Over the summer of 1956–57, new baths were finally built, at a cost of £13,400, and opened on a cold, wet April day. At last the baths were not very far from the hotel, the spring water being pumped across the Maruia River, into a 12 x 6 m swimming pool and 2 private pools. Changing sheds and toilets were also provided.

The old bathhouses were demolished at the same time and the suspension bridge was now used only to carry the pipeline from the springs to the baths. The days of filling your bath by bucket were over. The hotel was finished and given a liquor licence. Now that the new baths were in a sunny position, Maruia Springs showed a much kindlier face than had been the case for almost 100 years.

But problems still beset this remote area. In August of 1957 most of the galvanised iron across the swing bridge was split by frost. The replacement was provided with draining points so that the pipe could be emptied when a flow of water was not required. Floods threatened to wash away both bridge and pipeline in 1967, forcing the Government to spend £3,580 on protection works. A landmark disappeared in February 1968 when the Maruia Springs Hotel was destroyed by fire.

The Tourist Department withdrew its interests in Maruia Springs in November 1971, at the same time as it withdrew from Te Puia and Morere, areas with similar isolation and accommodation problems.

The Snoline Spa Hotel, which replaced the 1930s building, is a centre for South Island tourism, especially as one end of the St James Walkway connects with the Lewis Pass Road, close to the hotel. The 1957 baths have been extended and upgraded, for the use of hotel guests, passing motorists and thankful trampers.

References

1   Frank Moorhouse, Inspector, to T. E. Donne, Superintendent, Department of Tourist and Health Resorts, 2 August 1902. Tourist Department file 1902/111.
2   Mineral water sample 9377, Maruia Springs, J. S. Maclaurin, Government Analyst, in reply to letter of 28 August 1902. Tourist Department file 1902/111.
3   *Reefton Herald*, 19 May 1904.
4   J. L. Thomson, District Surveyor, to W. G. Murray, Chief Surveyor, Nelson, 4 July 1902. Tourist Department file 1902/111.
5   *Ibid.*
6   John McNee, Hon. Secretary of the Murchison League, 21 July 1904.
7   A. S. Wohlmann, Government Balneologist, to Acting Superintendent of Department of Tourist and Health Resorts, 6 August 1904.
8   *The Colonist*, 14 March 1905.
9   *Ibid.*
10 *The Kumara Times*, 7 March 1905.
11 T. E. Donne, Superintendent, to Minister for Tourist and Health Resorts, 6 September 1906.
12 *Christchurch Press*, 7 March 1905.
13 Extract from Chief Clerk's report, 6 May 1925. Tourist Department file 1920/12.
14 *Ibid.*
15 S. J. Collett, General Manager, Department of Tourist and Health Resorts, to Private Secretary to the Minister, 6 July 1925.
16 W. Clinkard, General Manager, to the Minister of Tourist and Health Resorts, 22 May 1930. Tourist Department file 1920/12.
17 S. J. Morris, Reefton, to General Manager, Department of Tourist and Health Resorts, 26 September 1906.
18 *Otago Daily Times*, 8 January 1931.
19 *Westport News*, 11 January 1932.
20 G. W. Clinkard, General Manager, to Minister of Tourist and Health Resorts and Publicity, 15 March 1932. Tourist Department file 1920/12.
21 *Nelson Evening Mail*, 21 May 1943.
22 J. K. McAlpine to the Hon. W. A. Bodkin, Minister of Internal Affairs, 2 April 1952. Tourist Department file 20/12.

12 Wairakei

Neither of Robert Graham's 2 spas, Waiwera and Wairakei, would be recognised as such today by a European visitor — the first would be seen as a recreational pool complex, the second as a tourist hotel with geothermal bathing. In their heyday, however, both had some of the features of their Northern Hemisphere counterparts, despite their lack of special diets, medical staff, electrical apparatus and steam or vapour baths.

Like Waiwera, Wairakei was selected by businessman Graham for its climate, its atmosphere, its scenery and its access to recreational activities. The area provided hot mineral water for drinking and bathing, and there was comfortable, if unusual, accommodation well suited to the convalescent patient.

Robert Graham insisted that Wairakei's climate was different from Taupo's. At 405 m above sea level, the air was very clear and because the area was over the lip of the rise from Lake Taupo, it was sheltered from the cold southerly winds that cross the lake from the 3 central North Island mountains.

Visitors were encouraged to make walking and riding excursions from the Wairakei Hotel to the Geyser Valley, the Aratiatia Rapids, the Huka Falls, and the Karapiti Blowhole. The Geyser House, as the hotel was called, was advertised as a hydropathic hotel. Before he came out to New Zealand, Scotsman Robert Graham doubtless had some knowledge of hydropathic institutions such as Strathpeffer or Crieff. Advertisements for Wairakei in Rotorua's *Hot Lakes Chronicle* emphasised "all the comforts of a home for tourists and invalids".[1] For a short period Robert Graham heralded the development of tourist hotel chains in this century. Apart from hotels in Auckland, he had one at Waiwera, the Lake House at Ohinemutu, the Geyser House at Wairakei and the Rotomahana Hotel at Tarawera. Robert Graham knew where to place his hotels; the Rotomahana accommodated most of the tourists going to the famous Pink and White Terraces.

Had Graham lived longer, Wairakei would undoubtedly have become more of a spa than was the case after he died in 1885. He had only 4 years in which to develop the property. His 1881 purchase of 1897 ha in the area was probably one of the main reasons for passing Thermal Springs Districts Act in the same year. His acquisition went through the Land Court only 6 months before the Act came into force; after that, Maori landowners in thermal springs areas could sell land only to the Government.

The main result of the Act was the creation of the Government town of Rotorua, but the legislation also prevented men like Robert Graham from making

(NEAR TAUPO).

THE undersigned begs to inform invalids and others visiting the Hot Springs, that he has opened an establishment at Wairakei, for the treatment of

RHEUMATIC AFFECTIONS & DISORDERS OF THE NERVOUS SYSTEM.

The extraordinary efficacy of the Wairakei mineral waters for the cure of Rheumatic and Spinal Complaints, and other diseases of a kindred nature has induced him, after an examination of the various springs of the Lake District, to fix upon Wairakei as the spot, above all others, where the thermal waters possess the most reliable properties.

The Kiriohinekai hot spring, which has for many years been known to the natives for its extraordinary curative properties, and will be the principal water used. In this spring the "Water Fall," "Fountain," and "Cascade Baths" form natural bathing pools; and arrangements have been made by which invalids will receive every attention during the treatment of their complaints.

DR. CAMPBELL, of Taupo, will visit **Wairakei** when required.

K. D. SYKES,
HYDROPATHIST.

An 1884 advertisement for Wairakei. Robert Graham was a spa pioneer for this country in many ways — the first European style spa at Waiwera, the first marketing of mineral waters from Waiwera, at Wairakei the first hydropathic specialist (10 years before Te Aroha and Hanmer; Rotorua never had such a person). *Graham's Guide to the Hot Lakes of New Zealand, Auckland Institute and Museum Library.*

private developments of hot springs areas. Critics of the Act, who felt that it was wrong for the Government to have a monopoly over thermal areas, could point to Robert Graham's Waiwera as being the most successful of the nineteenth-century New Zealand spas. Although they overlooked Waiwera's great advantage — its proximity to the largest city — it is interesting all the same to wonder what Robert Graham might have done with Rotorua's Sulphur Point.

He would have had difficulties with the acidic waters but, being a practical man, he may well have considered it insane to pipe corrosive waters into a magnificent building like the Rotorua Baths. One thing is certain — he would have constructed an attractive hotel close to the baths. The Sanatorium at Rotorua offered only spartan accommodation. To make it like a European spa, the place badly needed a hotel on the grand Waiwera scale, with special features such as Waiwera's lift for crippled invalids and Miss Graham's determined regime of recreation.

Certainly, during the 4 years of Graham's direction of Wairakei, the establishment seemed to be moving towards a style of institution different from the one his family sold in 1919, when the primary concerns were the scenic attractions of the Geyser Valley and the Huka Falls. By 1895, 10 years after Graham's death, an advertisement in the Rotorua *Hot Lakes Chronicle* devoted 3 lines to Wairakei's hydropathic advantages and 24 to describing the general scenery. In 1882, by contrast, *The New Guide to the Lakes and Hot Springs* described Robert Graham's plans to establish "a proper hydropathic hospital at Wairakei, under care and management of a thoroughly competent hydropathist".[2] (Hydrotherapy had become an obsession in Europe at the time Graham migrated to New Zealand.)

Among the raw material the entrepreneur had at his disposal at Wairakei were 4 junctions of hot and cold water. The natural advantages of these streams meant there was no need for the difficult plumbing involved at Rotorua where, as the level of the lake sank lower, the Priest Bath had to be excavated more and more deeply. The main resource, and the one that gave the Wairakei spa its fame, was the Kiriohinekai Stream. The name, meaning food for the skin of a young woman, shows that the local Tuwharetoa people had christened the stream for its smoothening effect on the skin. Like the Madam Rachel pool at Rotorua, the Wairakei water left a deposit of silica on the skin, producing a temporary smoothness. Mrs Charles Dudley Robert Ward, writing as Thorpe Talbot, believed that the Kiriohinekai Stream affected hair, darkening it and promoting its growth. She suggested selling the water as a hair restorer.

Near Wairakei was a pool with an even more remarkable reputation. This was Matarakutia, which the Tuwharetoa used to cure leprosy, known to the Maori as ngerengere. When the second Medical Officer in charge of the baths at Rotorua investigated this disease in New Zealand, he found that many Maoris believed it was passed on deliberately, like a curse.[3] They knew it was necessary to give an intended victim something that belonged to a sufferer; they mistook the contagion of microbes for something magical. Some people, including the Rev. Richard Taylor, assumed the disease had something to do with the acid waters of the Plateau. They were probably confusing a locality of contagion with unusual phenomena of the area.

The original development of the Kiriohinekai Stream, in the 1880s. Robert Graham is standing at the left. He planned to develop Wairakei into a great spa. *Photograph by Frank Coxhead, Hocken Library.*

The Matarakutia Pool was not used for general bathing but the Kiriohinekai, which flowed from a blue lake called Pirorirori, was modified in places to make attractive baths. For some unexplained reason the lake was bulldozed out of existence in the 1960s, but the stream still flows out of the earth. In Robert Graham's day, from its source to its junction with the Waikato River, the stream averaged 32.2 to 43.3°C, and 3 baths were developed along its course. The Waterfall Bath, later known as the Fairy Bath, was even more attractive than any of the waterfall pools that still exist in the Waiotapu area.

Thorpe Talbot was considerably impressed with Robert Graham's energy: "Thousands of planted trees of all varieties are already thriving in their new locality . . . That is one point in which the owner excels most pioneers — he begins by beautifying. He aims at securing comfort and luxury for the future . . . From all that one has seen of Mr Graham's enterprise in this country, one judges his energy to be unlimited."[4] Sadly, he was dead 3 years later.

She went on to describe the future town of Wairakei, as Graham planned it. It was to have wide streets, extensive parks, fountains and recreation grounds. Every house was to have hot and cold water laid on in pipes. (This last idea preceded by 60 years a 1940 Government plan to have geothermal water reticulated through Rotorua houses.) In his own guide published in 1884 Graham announced that the town of Wairakei had been surveyed, complete "with pleasure-gardens, racecourse and cricket-fields".[5]

Wairakei, c. 1885 — the dining room of Robert Graham's other spa. It was not as successful as Waiwera because of its distance from large population centres. Such interior photographs of raupo and rush buildings are rare. *Hocken Library*.

Quite a different picture of Wairakei was given in 1884 by the Union Steamship Company's guide, *Maoriland*:

Mr R. Graham's establishment, consisting of a raupo cottage, partitioned off into comfortable bedrooms, and a wooden building just now in the course of erection to supplement the cottage. The surrounding ground looks at present somewhat bleak and barren, the trees that have been planted presenting rather a stunted appearance, and the grass refusing to take kindly to the inhospitable soil.[6]

In the 1880s the raupo and thatch hotel was unique in the country. The author of *Three in a Coach* remarked on its unusual appearance:

As we approached we were struck by what appeared to be a large haystack, and as the land round about certainly looked anything but fertile this was rather surprising. Still more were we surprised when we . . . saw smoke issuing from the stack. We were reassured when we saw the smoke issued from a chimney and that this eccentric haystack was furthermore furnished with windows. It was in fact a hotel, a low building of thatch in which are the tourists' dining-room, bedrooms and kitchen.[7]

After her husband's death in 1885, Mrs Graham (later remarried as Mrs Grierson) had the hotel considerably enlarged in 1897. It was built on the European chalet system, with small detached buildings. As Margaret Bullock wrote in 1899, "One of the chief charms of Wairakei is its homelike appearance. Instead of a big staring hotel the visitor finds tastefully laid out grounds and picturesque cottages."[8] The swimming bath near the hotel was known in the

This, the Fairy Pool, photographed about 1905, was one of several pools in the Kiriohinekai Stream. Some bathers claimed this water renewed their skin. *Photograph by Frank Radcliffe, Auckland Public Library Photograph Collection.*

1890s, and early this century, as the Mermaids' Bath. The stream flowed through it and weeping willows hung over the water.

A brochure published in 1905 and written by a Dr Alle of Napier listed Wairakei's advantages as a spa:

> It is sheltered from the cold winds of the south by a range of hills; the soil is so loose that no moisture can lodge on the surface. The Hotel faces the north, so that it obtains the benefit of the sunshine all day long . . . It is as a health resort for the invalid or tired business man that I consider Wairakei so eminently suitable.[9]

Furthermore, because the Wairakei water contained alum in solution, probably combined with silica, it had the astringent healing effects of ordinary alum salts without their drying and roughening action.

The Government Balneologist decided in the same year that some of the Wairakei waters might prove useful "for internal administration". He added, "somewhere in the neighbourhood is an Arsenical Spring . . . which might prove extremely valuable".[10] The estate of 1897 ha, including half the Geyser Valley, was offered to the Government in 1910 for £30,000. Unfortunately, the Government had just spent £40,000 on the Rotorua Bathhouse and was nervous of developing any other spas.

Among the minutiae of memos in the records of the Department of Tourist and Health resorts, there are a few extraordinary letters. One concerning Wairakei

This 1920 photograph showing the Kiriohinekai Stream flowing through the hotel bath is of the same area depicted in the 1880s photograph earlier in the chapter. *Alexander Turnbull Library*.

received in 1915, from a Mr Fell, had a note of national emergency, entreating that something be done quickly "to prevent, if possible, the group of Hot Springs . . . known as Wairakei from falling into the hands of an American Syndicate . . . there are unique supplies of most valuable chemical products being continually ejected from these springs which ought to be under Government control . . . and if these things are exploited and monopolised by speculators for private gain it will be a kind of disaster." The writer was particularly concerned about "a substance called in commerce anti-phlogiston . . . which is ejected at a certain place at Wairakei in the form of black mud . . . This substance used to cost 17s 6d per 1 lb now it costs £2.10s."[11] The material mentioned was made only in Germany and the urgency of Mr Fell's approach can be understood in the light of nationalist feeling during the First World War.

The Government was unmoved by Mr Fell's plea and a company calling itself Wairakei Ltd purchased the area in 1919. In *Wairakei the Wonderful* brochures, put out in 1919 and 1934, the waters and the baths were very much emphasised, but the Second World War saw, to a great extent, the end of Wairakei as a spa. From September 1942 until September 1946 the hotel was taken over by the Mental Hospitals Department and used for patients from Porirua Hospital which had been damaged by an earthquake. During this period the buildings became shabby and it was some time before the area reverted to being an attractive tourist resort. A large fire in the district further spoiled the appearance of Wairakei.

Wairakei was bought by the Tourist Department in 1946 and the renovated hotel was reopened in 1949. It was regarded by the department as a tourist hotel rather than a spa. Now part of the Tourist Hotel chain, the hotel has 2 modern swimming pools, heated by steam. The Kiriohinekai Stream is no longer used.

ROTORUA

AND NEW ZEALAND'S THERMAL WONDERLAND

An example of the Department of Tourist and Publicity's attractive brochures of the 1930s. Unfortunately by that time the enormous maintenance problem of the Rotorua Bathhouse was diminishing Government interest in spas. The illustration is from a painting by Leonard Mitchell. *Rotorua Museum.*

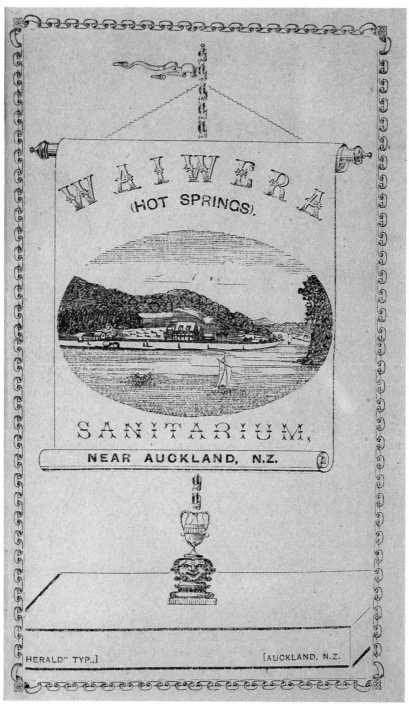

New Zealand's first spa brochure, 1875. This was another first for Robert Graham who established the first European-style spa in the country. *Auckland Institute and Museum.*

The Rotorua Bathhouse c. 1909. This building symbolised the New Zealand Government's intention to create a spa of international significance in order to attract more tourists to this country. *Rotorua Museum*.

Until the 1970s Te Aroha water was the most popular mineral or table water in the country. The No. 15 and the No. 8 springs were both used commercially as early as the 1880s. The No. 8 had an octagonal pumproom and was known in the 1890s as the Onslow Spring, after the Governor-General of that time. *National Archives*.

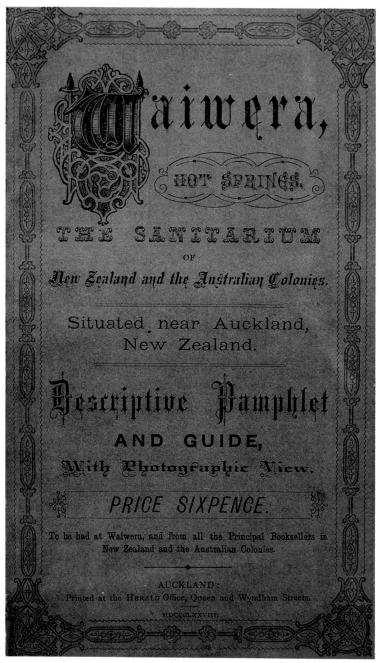

Waiwera,

HOT SPRINGS.

THE SANITARIUM

OF

New Zealand and the Australian Colonies.

Situated near Auckland,
New Zealand.

Descriptive Pamphlet

AND GUIDE,

With Photographic View.

PRICE SIXPENCE.

To be had at Waiwera, and from all the Principal Booksellers in
New Zealand and the Australian Colonies.

AUCKLAND:
Printed at the HERALD Office, Queen and Wyndham Streets.

MDCCCLXXVIII.

Robert Graham's 1878 guide for his spa at Waiwera was the second to be published for the resort. This brochure was distributed in Australia as well as throughout New Zealand. When the Government published popular guides to Rotorua, Hanmer and Te Aroha, overseas distribution was limited to Tourist Department Agencies and a few doctors in Australia and London. *Auckland Institute and Museum*

Maruia Springs in 1985. The Snoline Spa Hotel, which replaced the original hotel, is renovating and enlarging the bath facilities at the Lewis Pass resort. *Wilton and Gore Limited, Snoline Spa Hotel.*

Since 1970 the AC Baths at Taupo have been 1 of the largest thermal water complexes in the country. The private baths are fed from the spring that was used by the Armed Constabulary in the 1880s. *Taupo Borough Council.*

The new appearance of Waiwera — the Choob Tower at Hartley Hot Pools. There are also pools designed for barbecues and other social functions. The resort is a good example of how an old spa became an important recreation centre. *Hartley Consolidated Limited.*

Miranda at the bottom of the Hauraki Gulf or what was called the Firth of Thames has probably the largest hot swimming pool in the country — 45 m long by 15 m wide. Unlike many hot baths, it contains pure mineral water, constantly replaced by a flow of 9000 gallons per hour, rising from springs. *Photography by G. Kidd, Miranda Hot Springs Oasis.*

Opal Hot Springs, Okauia, near Matamata, in the 1980s. Close to the main baths is a very attractive private bath built around the main spring, known as Ramaroa. *Cleaver family, Opal Hot Springs.*

The water slides at Waingaro Hot Springs, near Ngaruawahia. Waingaro and Miranda are examples of hot springs which were once rather isolated but are now, with modern transport and good roads, very popular. The modern complex at Waingaro began in 1977. *Pilling family, Waingaro Thermal Baths.*

The Blue Baths, Rotorua, 1933. The Roman pillars, crescent windows and the woman's dress suggest an element of luxury important for an international spa. *Rotorua Museum*.

Wairakei was too close to the Government's investment in Rotorua for the Tourist Department to want to spend a great deal of money on a rival attraction. Without the entrepreneurial genius of a Robert Graham the place had too many access difficulties to become a great spa. The pumice roads of the Plateau were a nightmare for many travellers in both summer and winter, with dust clouds and axle-breaking pot holes. The early tourist cars which served as buses on the Plateau had to carry spare springs and drivers often had to replace axles in scrub-land 30 or 40 km from a town. Rotorua and Waiwera succeeded because of ease of access, by rail and ship. It is possible that, had he lived, Graham might have persuaded Government or private interests to link Taupo by rail. Had that happened there would undoubtedly have been a small station at Wairakei, or at least a coach service to a nearby station, as was the case with Okoroire. But none of this happened and Robert Graham's dream of a true spa town never became a reality.

References

1   *Hot Lakes Chronicle*, file for 1895, Rotorua Museum.
2   Talbot, Thorpe [pseudonym for Mrs Charles Dudley Robert Ward]. *The New Guide to the Lakes and Hot Springs, and a month in hot water*, Wilson & Horton, 1882.
3   Ginders, Alfred. Leprosy among the Maoris at Taupo and Rotorua. *Appendices to the Journal of the House of Representatives*, 1890 G-5.
4   Talbot, Thorpe. *op. cit.*
5   Graham, Robert Jnr. *Graham's Guide to the Hot Lakes of New Zealand, Pink and White Terraces, Wairakei Geysers, Huka Falls and Waiwera Hot Springs*, Auckland, Wilson & Horton, 1884.
6   Wilson, A. *Maoriland, an illustrated handbook of New Zealand, by A. Wilson and others*. Wellington, Union S.S. Co., 1884.
7   *Three in a Coach. A descriptive account of a tour through the hot lakes and geysers district of the North Island*, Christchurch, The Press, 1891.
8   Bullock, Margaret. *Wonderland: a glimpse at the marvels and beauties of the Taupo volcanic zone, New Zealand*, Government Printer, 1899.
9   Alle, F. H. J. "A Testimonial" in J. S. G. *Overland Route to Wairakei from Auckland South and from Wellington North*, Christchurch Press, 1909.
10 Government Balneologist to Superintendent, Department of Tourist and Health Resorts, 28 July 1905. Tourist Department file 1903/31.
11 C. Y. Fell, Nelson, to Manager, Department of Tourist and Health Resorts, 22 February 1915. Tourist Department file 1903/31.

13 Taupo

There are many areas of geothermal activity around Taupo and all but 2 of them have had a history of bathing. Only at Rotokawa, with its very stark landscape, and at the Okurawai mudpool area, better known to tourists as "The Craters of the Moon", is there no suitable bathing water.

For nineteenth-century travellers, the most popular bathing area in the southern half of the Volcanic Plateau was at the site of the present Spa Hotel. Most of the early baths were found in a sheltered natural amphitheatre where a hot and a cold stream converged. Some of the very earliest improvements to natural pools were near the junction of this combined stream with the Waikato River.

It is a picturesque area with its steaming cliffs, varied thermal activity and the curious U-shaped valleys that are typical of some volcanic areas. Because of the shelter, and the warmth provided by blue chloride pools, ferns are found here that will not grow in exposed areas of the Plateau. Some of the photographs taken in the 1880s by George Valentine and Alfred Burton caught the difference between this valley and the more exposed areas of the Volcanic Plateau. At the time of Alfred Burton's visit the valley was called The Glen. Its original name was Tapapa Kuao and the hot stream is the Otumuheke.

The natural pools were modified after an Armed Constabulary redoubt was established at Taupo in 1869 and after a hotel was built and a regular coach run from Napier started in 1872. This service opened up the Volcanic Plateau to Napier, which was a comparatively large town in the 1870s. The following advertisement appeared in the *Hawke's Bay Herald*, in September 1872: "The use of the convenient baths and dressing-rooms just designed with great taste and erected by Mr McMurray, distant 1¼ miles from the hotel, may be had on application to, and arrangement with the proprietor."[1]

This was 10 years before the Government bathhouse was built in the Sulphur Point area of Rotorua. During the 1870s Taupo township and the little Ohinemutu settlement at Rotorua were very similar in size and facilities. In the 1880s Government development in the latter area meant that Rotorua and not Taupo became the main centre of the Plateau, and the gap widened in the 1890s when Rotorua was linked to the railway system, and Taupo was not. The difference between the 2 centres was reflected in bathing facilities in subsequent years. What was unique and cosy in Taupo in the 1880s became outdated. This was particularly so with the Armed Constabulary Baths, commonly known as the AC

The Glen at Taupo in 1885. Two baths can be seen, on either side of the Ngati Tarawhai carving; John Loffley stands to the left of the carving and the Otumuheke Stream flows beneath him. *Photograph by Burton Bros, National Museum.*

Baths. In Rotorua, by contrast, the Government periodically replaced bathhouses in its attempt to make the town a spa of international significance.

The Hawke's Bay *Herald* described McMurray's bath in 1873.

> The Crow's Nest [a famous geyser on the right bank of the Waikato] and surrounding objects have lately been bought from the natives by McMurray, who has already so far utilised his purchase as to erect a small bathhouse on a convenient portion of it, and to cut a pretty zig-zag approach to the spot which is probably half a mile nearer the hotel than Lofley's [this was the Glen, developed by John Loffley]. The building is on the banks of the Waikato and consists of one good-sized room. It contains a wooden bath, supplied on the one hand with hot water through a brass tap and on the other, by means of a small pump, with cold water from the river . . . After the hot bath, he or she as the case may be, can then open a door on the river side and take an agreeable plunge — thus effectively guarding against cold, such as the relaxed state of the system on leaving the hot bath may be supposed to induce.[2]

The same article mentioned developments in the rival establishment in the Glen. Mr Loffley, variously known as "Jack", "John" and "Edward", was a former member of the Armed Constabulary, who had married the daughter of a chief who owned Tapapa Kuao. When the *Herald* reporter called Mr Loffley was busy erecting a roof and sides over his bath "so as to enable ladies to enjoy privacy".[3]

There was another attractive pool at the junction of the Otumuheke with the Waikato. J. Ernest Tinne wrote in *The Wonderland of the Antipodes*, 1873, that "the modus operandi was to climb up a little waterfall, shoot down the smooth rock channel . . . into the pool beneath, then recline for an interval in the comfortable

The earliest photograph of Taupo's spa taken soon after Sir William Fox's visit in 1874. Loffley's bathhouse is at the junction of a hot and a cold stream, with his whare at the right. The first frame building is being erected. The valley was known as Tapapakuao, but was later called the Glen, and then the Spa. *Alexander Turnbull Library.*

stone chair formed by nature enjoying a douche or shower bath".[4] The author claimed that, even at the time of his visit, before the regular coach run from Napier, the hot stream already had a reputation in Hawke's Bay.

One of the most interesting of all travellers' accounts of the Volcanic Plateau was that of a German doctor, Max Büchner. His *Reise durch den Stillen Ozean*, published in 1878, contained a delightful description of the Glen in 1876:

> The miniature valley seemed more attractive than the bare plateau, over which a chilly wind was blowing. The scenery became more idyllic the further I went. Features of this charming, peaceful little spot include a dovecot of woven reeds, two or three low huts of the same material, and grazing sheep, luxurious vegetation and steep walls of rock, high enough to offer protection against the cold wind.[5]

He met Loffley's wife — "a pretty young Maori woman approached in such a scanty garment that I almost beat a retreat, apologising" — and felt that the couple "represented the god and goddess of the wonderful healing springs. European reserve is incompatible with such a mythological calling, hence the simplicity of their costumes".[6] Loffley wore the shawl which had been a favoured garment with the Armed Constabulary.

Büchner described how the springs united to form a broad stream, 1 m deep, which flowed through flax. The roof of the natural bath was made of plaited reeds, and from this, honeysuckle hung over the water. A rush hut served as the changing room, with a notice inside it explaining that baths cost 1 shilling. The author also found a beautiful natural pool near the Waikato: "This could have been competition for Mr Jack and he had therefore filled it up with rubbish".[7]

Sir William Fox, artist, and at one stage Premier of New Zealand, was impressed with Loffley's Glen. In a proposal to Vogel, who was then Premier, Fox suggested giving Loffley a lease on the area, as "the Government has extinguished the Native title to the locality".[8] The lease was to be conditional upon Loffley constructing baths and providing cottages for invalids or tourists. The Government acted upon the proposal and Loffley was given a lease.

Fox was the first to paint the Glen, in 1874, but no illustration exists of McMurray's Bath, which had gone out of use by that date. McMurray had not found it a paying proposition, but Loffley was a very good touter and persuaded most Taupo tourists to visit his Glen.

Chantrey Harris, writing in 1878, was the first to mention Loffley's area in a guide book. He visited the sources of the streams which were the sites of future bathhouses: "The water bubbles up from rocky faces, which in the case of the hot stream is encrusted with mineral deposits".[9] This rocky face can still be seen behind the AC Baths in Taupo. The guide book also noted the curious sensation experienced at the junction of the hot and cold streams, where bathers felt cool water on their lower limbs and hot water at the surface. (Bathers at the Waitangi Soda Springs, Rotoehu, can also experience this contrast.) Chantrey Harris's book also mentioned that the Government was constructing a road from the town of Taupo to the Glen. This was 3 years before such work was begun in Rotorua.

In 1880 another small bathhouse was built at the cliff face by the Armed Constabulary. Hina Fletcher, in her *Tales of Early Taupo*, claims that the reason for its construction was a disagreement between the Armed Constabulary men and John Loffley.[10] Apparently Loffley increased the price of beer at the Glen but the Constabulary men refused to pay the extra. They were then told they couldn't use Loffley's baths, so they built their own. It is just as likely, however, that it resulted from a visit by Rolleston, Minister of Lands and Survey. He was to some extent responsible for the early development at Te Aroha in 1880, at Rotorua in 1881 and Hanmer in 1883. Because most of the relevant Lands and Survey files have been destroyed, it is difficult to know how involved Rolleston was, but it is possible that he was as much the father of New Zealand spas as Thomas E. Donne or Sir Joseph Ward.

The Armed Constabulary excavated the rock where the spring emerged from the cliff, lined the area with timber slabs and built dressing sheds. The spring of the other hot tributary of the Otumuheke Stream, the Sulphur Bath, which also had an Armed Constabulary bathhouse built over it, was visited by the author of *Three in a Coach* in 1891:

> We groped our way through the copsewood that fills the uncultivated part of the glen . . . A small shed has been built over the stream where the sulphur spring rises; and the bath itself is contained in a coffin-like trough. The water was so hot we remained in but a moment; it was long enough, however, to incrust the skin with a thin coating of sulphur that made you feel like a two-legged lucifer match.[11]

The original Armed Constabulary Baths at Taupo, 1885. The present AC complex is in this valley. The photograph shows the starkness of the Volcanic Plateau in the nineteenth century. *Photograph by Burton Bros, National Museum.*

Most visitors to Taupo bathed at the Glen. Pownall, in his *Illustrated Guide to the West Coast of the North Island*, wrote of the respect which travellers felt for Loffley himself — "the landlord, guide, counsellor, and friend of all tourists or invalids who seek his abode in search of pleasure or health." To Pownall, and other visitors, Loffley's "wit and fund of stories [kept] up the spirits of many, who from the weakness consequent upon failing health, would otherwise be apt to give way to feelings of despondency."[12]

The lease of the valley was transferred in 1888 and Loffley's Glen became Joshua's Spa. John Joshua bought a carved house, Tiki-a-Tamamutu, from a chief at Oruanui, north-west of Taupo. It was shifted to the valley where it was used as a dining room, and later, a lounge. Under Joshua's care the baths were enlarged, as was the AC Bath, which came under his lease. He locked it up for the use of his patrons — to the irritation of Taupo citizens. His spa offered something unique in New Zealand. Under one of the bridges over the stream was a hot sulphur spring. Hot water from this could be taken directly to the bedroom of an invalid too ill to go to the baths.

The third lessee, Gallagher, who took over in 1895, replaced the stream baths with other buildings. One was known as the Kathleen Bath, after one daughter, and the Sulphur Spring became the Cathrine (*sic*) Spring, presumably after another daughter. What was built originally as the women's bathhouse, around 1900, survived to be the only bathhouse at the spa by 1940. It was replaced by an open air pool after 1975, and also more recently, by an enclosed pool.

Ngati Tarawhai carvings adorned the bathhouse at the Spa, Taupo. The Otumuheke River flowed through it. *Photograph by Winkelmann, Auckland Institute and Museum.*

The AC Bath, managed by a domain board from the late 1890s, was rebuilt in 1900; the replacement was described as "a building of the crudest descriptions".[13] When the Taupo Borough Council took over from the board, new baths were constructed in 1954, and very much enlarged in 1970. At the present AC complex only the private pools use mineral water. Heated fresh water is used in the very large lido pool and in the other facilities, which include a sauna.

There is another area of natural hot water in Taupo that has been used for bathing over several centuries. The first European to be interested in its possibilities was Sir William Fox. In a letter to Vogel in 1874, he described its setting:

At the distance of a mile from the Constabulary post and township, along the eastern shore of the lake, a warm stream, a yard or two wide, crosses the road and meanders into the lake. Following it inland by a Maori track, a narrow gorge is reached, in which the small stream expands into two considerable pools, varying in depth from a few inches to several feet. They are both of considerable temperature, and a favourite resort of the neighbouring Natives.[14]

Raupo and rushes on their banks made the pools hard to reach and Fox felt a lot of work would be needed to make them "a place of general resort".[15]

The development came in 1889 when a Mr Ross built the Terrace Hotel above the pools. The terrace was a black sinter slope, known as the Black Terrace, at the head of the valley. Mr Ross so far improved this valley, known as Onekeneke, that the 1894 Willis's guide book described the hot lake, created out of the 2 pools, as "the finest natural swimming bath in the Thermal District".[16] At the foot of the lake was a spout bath and at its head the Iron Bath, supplied from the Black

The Onekeneke Valley and the serpentine lake. The little bathhouse at the end of the valley was known as the Iron Bath. To the right was the black sinter slope from which the Terrace Hotel took its name. *Photograph by R. Thompson, Rotorua Art Gallery Collection..*

Terrace Springs. This valley is still one of the most pleasant areas of the Volcanic Plateau. The Terrace Hotel, now De Bretts, on its high ridge has a magnificent view over Lake Taupo. The Onekeneke Valley behind it is sheltered from the southerly winds which sweep across the lake in July and August. The modern pool complex fits neatly and unobtrusively into the landscape.

For most of this century, however, the AC Baths were the most commonly used bathing place for Taupo citizens. A town water supply was not available until 1960 and the AC Baths became the communal bathing centre, where people armed with towel and soap, waited for up to 2 hours to have a bath. Twice there were attempts to have water brought down from the AC Spring or the Sulphur Spring so that a hot water bath could be built on the lakeside domain, next to the main street. In 1929 it looked as though Taupo might be developed by the Government, in the same way as Rotorua. Unfortunately for Taupo, Sir Joseph Ward, a spa enthusiast, died the following year and the Depression put a stop to further plans. The next attempt failed because of the Second World War. It was largely local effort that created the present AC complex.

The parkland of planted trees around the sauna and lido pool make a marked contrast to the Taupo Dr Büchner described 110 years ago: "This outpost of European culture is a desert devoid of population. No craft lends life to the wide green expanse of the lake whose waves beat monotonously on the muddy banks. There's not a tree to be seen".[17]

98

De Brett's Hotel thermal complex at Taupo. The 1960s redevelopment of the Onekeneke Valley blends in with the landscape. The hotel, formerly the Terrace, has a magnificent view over the lake. *Rotorua Museum.*

References

1   *Hawke's Bay Herald*, 25 September 1872.
2   *Hawke's Bay Herald*, 27 February 1873.
3   *Ibid.*
4   Tinne, J. Ernest. *The Wonderland of the Antipodes; and other sketches of travel in the North Island of New Zealand*, London, Sampson Low, 1873.
5   Büchner, Max. *Reise durch den Stillen Ozean*, Breslau, 1878.
6   *Ibid.*
7   *Ibid.*
8   Fox, the Hon. W. "Hot springs district of the North Island" (letter to the Hon. the Premier). *Appendices to the Journal of the House of Representatives*, 1874 H-26.
9   Harris, J. Chantrey. *The Southern Guide to the Hot Lakes District of the North Island of New Zealand*, Dunedin, Daily Times, 1878.
10   Fletcher, H. M. *Tales of Early Taupo*, Taupo, 1980.
11   *Three in a Coach: a descriptive account of a tour through the hot lakes and geysers district of the North Island*, Christchurch, The Press, 1891.
12   Pownall, R. W. *Illustrated Guide to the West Coast of the North Island, N.Z.*, Wanganui, Willis, 1885.
13   Clerk of the Taupo Domain Board to General Manager, Department of Tourist and Health Resorts, 5 October 1932.
14   Fox, the Hon. W. *op. cit.*
15   *Ibid.*
16   Allen, George. *Willis's Guide Book of New Routes for Tourists*, Wanganui, Willis, 1894.
17   Büchner, Max. *op. cit.*

14 Tokaanu

Travellers who stayed at Okoroire could imagine they were at a British spa, but those who visited Tokaanu were in no doubt that they were on the Volcanic Plateau of New Zealand. It was not just the obvious evidence of volcanoes and thermal activity, it was the fact that, at Tokaanu, there was no deliberate attempt to create a spa. People used the hot springs for medicinal purposes; the water in one of the pools, Torotiti, was a centuries' old cure for ailments. There were hotels at Tokaanu and it was on the tourist route. Both its setting at the southern end of Lake Taupo and its steamer service could have helped to make it a picturesque and pleasant spa, but apart from some concreting and new paths, Tokaanu changed little during the great New Zealand spa years of 1880 to 1910. It continued to be a quiet little New Zealand town where travellers would stay a night or two and, almost incidentally, use the hot baths.

The hot springs at Tokaanu were much better known to nineteenth-century European travellers than most hot springs outside Rotorua. The artist G. F. Angas, an illustrator of the Taupo region in the 1840s, wrote of the hot springs at Waihi, close to Tokaanu: "The medicinal properties of these hot mineral springs preserve the natives in a healthy state, and render their skins beautifully smooth and clear."[1] The Austrian scientist, Ferdinand von Hochstetter, remarked that the hot creek, Te Atakokoreke, was a favourite bathing place.[2] This creek was the overflow of Torotiti, one of the most important pools in Tokaanu's thermal area.

William Fox wrote to the Premier, Julius Vogel, in 1874 to suggest that the Government develop the hot springs of the Volcanic Plateau. He considered Tokaanu an important part of that region, describing the main bathing pool as "convenient and peculiar".[3] It consisted of a deep centre, surrounded by a shelf a metre or 2 wide, on which the water was only 0.6 to 0.9 m deep. Fox envisaged Tokaanu as a significant centre once the road from the Volcanic Plateau to Wanganui was completed. As he suggested, it was logical to link the tourist attractions of the Volcanic Plateau with those of the Wanganui River.

Part of Fox's statement, however, pointed to the prejudice against the Maori which became noticeable early this century. He wrote: "The bathing facilities, however, at present, can only be used in common with the Natives, who morning to evening resort to the principal bath in such numbers as often to completely fill it". He warned that if the Maori landowners continued to occupy Tokaanu, "it would be necessary to utilise some of the other springs . . . for those who might prefer privacy to the communistic lavatory [the word is used in the old sense of a washing place] system of the Natives".[4] The spa at Sulphur Point,

Tokaanu in 1886. This area of waiariki (natural bathing pools) was admired by nineteenth-century Europeans. *Photograph by Burton Bros, National Museum.*

Rotorua, was developed in parallel with the historic and Maori-owned pools of nearby Ohinemutu. At Te Aroha and Te Puia separate bathhouses were built for the Maori people who formerly owned the springs, and at Morere Springs some of the first European bathers complained that Maoris tended to occupy the hot pools. In other areas, such as Waiwera, where great crowds of Maoris had once used the geothermal water, European purchase created a Pakeha enclave. This never happened at Tokaanu, where the Tuwharetoa people retained ownership of much of the thermal resource.

The Government made a fairly unsuccessful attempt at creating a town there in 1898; only a few of the allotments were taken up. An important part of the arrangements made between Percy Smith, acting for the Government, and the Tuwharetoa people of the area was that the latter were not to lose access to the main bathing pool. This agreement was later forgotten at one stage.

In 1900 a fence and changing sheds were erected around Marakerake Pool. By 1904 the Acting Superintendent of the Tourist Department was complaining to the Commissioner of Police of "nuisances being committed in the dressing shed".[5] But, as the district constable pointed out, the enclosure of the bath was on a native reserve and the Government had no claim or right to it. Percy Smith confirmed that Tuwharetoa access to Marakerake Pool had been a central issue in the agreement to establish a town at Tokaanu. Disagreement and friction lasted for some years. At one stage, in 1906, a hotel proprietor locked the Maori people out of the bath; a short while later the door was off its hinges.

101

This 1910 photograph shows the bathhouse built in the summer of 1900–01 at a cost of £500. It is really an enclosure around the natural pools. *Photograph by Lawrence Birks, Rotorua Museum.*

As an alternative, the Tourist Department built a concrete bath in 1910. Water was carried to it from the Torotiti Pool. With considerable understatement, the Director of Tourism wrote: "There is, I fear, a little irritation among the Natives over the erection of a new bathhouse for the use of Europeans or paying visitors".[6] A photograph of this bathhouse shows it looking more like a fort than a place of leisure, with its barbed wire-topped wall.

During the 1920s the hotelkeeper built a third bathhouse, only 400 m from the 1910 structure, purely for the use of his guests. The fact that the earlier bathhouse was leased to the hotelkeeper made it difficult for the Tourist Department to advertise Tokaanu's geothermal waters; advertisements for Tokaanu came to feature only trout fishing. The department's attitude to Tokaanu after 1910 could be summed up by the words of a 1935 letter from the General Manager, when he wrote that "the Reserve and the baths may be classed as one of the Department's responsibilities rather than an asset of substantial value or importance".[7]

The department solved its problem in 1936 by gazetting the area as a domain. This passed control back to the local people, although Government assistance was continued through the Lands and Survey Department, which made a grant of £600 in 1953 for new bathhouses. The Tourist Department's only interest in Tokaanu after 1936 was the hotel, which it bought in 1944.

The Tuwharetoa people made a gift of land to add to the domain, in memory of men from the area killed in the 2 World Wars. The Tokaanu Memorial Thermal Park, as the whole area is now called has, since 1981, been administered by the Lands and Survey Department. New baths and bathhouses were built in 1982. Only the private pools use water from the geothermal pools.

Just as Tokaanu seems to have been forgotten in recent times, with the development of Turangi, so it must have seemed in 1895 that Taupo village and Rotorua were attracting all attention on the Volcanic Plateau. Tokaanu was the one place where the original owners stated that they wished to be part of any development of the thermal pools, but the Government was not prepared to invest sufficient money to provide sophisticated baths and a caretaker. As a result tourists complained that the baths were not sufficiently cared for, while the local people felt that they had, to some extent, lost control of their heritage. If something like the present baths and park had existed in 1900, Tokaanu might have developed more like some of the small New Zealand spas. It is possible, however, that this might not have been what the local people wanted.

The newly developed Tokaanu Memorial Thermal Park and the new Tourist Hotel Corporation hotel will help restore Tokaanu to its former prominence as a geothermal bathing area.

References

1   Angas, G. F. *Savage Life and Scenes in Australia and New Zealand*. London, Smith, Elder, 1844.
2   Hochstetter, Ferdinand von. *New Zealand: Its physical geography, geology and natural history*, Stuttgart, Cotta, 1867.
3   Fox, the Hon. W. "Hot springs district of the North Island" (letter to the Hon. the Premier). *Appendices to the Journal of the House of Representatives*, 1874 H-26.
4   *Ibid*.
5   C. R. C. Robieson, Acting Superintendent, Department of Tourist and Health Resorts, 20 September 1904.
6   B. M. Wilson, Director, Department of Agriculture, Commerce and Tourists, to Minister of Tourist and Health Resorts, 26 November 1910. File 2/33.
7   General Manager to the Minister of Industries and Commerce, Tourist and Publicity, 1 May 1935. Tourist Department file 20/70.

15 Morere

Although less well known than other areas developed by the Tourist Department, Morere, set in an unusually attractive reserve, is one of the most picturesque of all New Zealand's hot springs areas. Forty km north-east of Wairoa and 60 km south-west of Gisborne, the springs rise in and along the banks of the Mangakawa Stream, which feeds the Tunanui, a tributary of the Nuhaka River. The Lands and Survey Department claimed that the Morere Springs were discovered in 1889 but the Ngati Kahungunu people have used them for centuries. Sadly, the history of these East Coast springs has been plagued by the problems of landslips and a limited hot water supply.

What first interested Lands and Survey, before the days of the Tourist Department, was the analysis of the Morere spring water. It contained more iodine than any other such water tested thus far. The Colonial Analyst claimed, in fact, that Morere's water resembled that of Germany's Wiesbaden spa and of England's Harrogate.

The water is unique in its extreme saltiness. The huge amount of iodides — 1700 times the quantity found in sea water — made the water so brown that bathers often thought it wasn't clean. People suffering from goitre drank Morere's special water; it was also drunk for the later stages of syphilis. The waters are now used for less desperate purposes.

Land was reserved around the springs in 1896 and an accommodation house was begun the following year. That the springs were already well known by that date can be assumed from the 1897 Crown Lands report: "At the Nuhaka hot springs . . . a large accommodation house is in the process of erection . . . so that next summer visitors will fare better than hitherto. A large number of people already make use of these springs for the benefit of their healing properties who have hitherto had to live in tents".[1] The 1899 report included a warning that the establishment was in its earliest stages. As though disclaiming responsibility, the Lands and Survey Department advised that the accommodation was under private management.

By 1901 the department reported that "great improvements have been made in the accommodation at the hotel, which is now comfortable",[2] but the proprietor found that few people would stay at his hotel, despite his "most proper accommodations", while there were no acceptable baths. There were primitive ones there from 1897, but the Nuhaka Settlers' Association considered that by 1901 they were "past redemption". They were, it claimed, dangerous because of large

The first Morere bathhouse, 1897, illustrates the lengths to which Victorian bathers were prepared to go for hot mineral water. It was at the top of a narrow valley subject to slips, and with no footpath. This scene contrasts with that of the No. 2 bathhouse, which had come under the civilising influence of the Tourist Department. *Alexander Turnbull Library*.

The first Government bathhouse, built in 1904, was lit by methane collected from the springs. The pool in the foreground was created by the run-off from the bathhouse. *Alexander Turnbull Library.*

rocks on the cliffs above the stream and bathing pools, as well as being unsanitary and "unsightly".[4]

A slip had filled the large bath and, as a result, the building had been roofed with slabs, but a heavy fall of earth would still be disastrous. East Coast hill country is a very unstable region in which to try and build in a gully; the clay, shingle and rock of the area are difficult to consolidate. The Morere stream and springs are in a narrow valley with steep cliffs, and comparatively safe sites for the bathhouses could be found only in the lower valley where there were no overhanging cliffs. Unfortunately, the springs are in the upper part of the valley and transporting the water involved 2 problems: temperature loss between source and bath, and the pipes' vulnerability to damage from slips.

Road communication was another problem. As with the other East Coast spring area at Te Puia, access was difficult. In 1902, his first year in New Zealand, the Government Balneologist, A. S. Wohlmann, must have found the district's roads a contrast to those around Bath, where he had been working at the famous spa. He recorded mud 1 m deep on his way to Morere, and had to bribe someone to get him to the springs. The roads in this area were often impassable between June and October. Faced with this, and then by baths filled in with slips, the Englishman could well have been amused by the locals' 1903 petition, which claimed that "The Morere Hot Springs are splendidly situated and adapted as a resort for invalids and tourists".[5]

Wohlmann did, however, think that Morere's setting was attractive, and advised that any development should retain the natural character of the place:

Morere, c. 1920. The No. 2 bathhouse was built further down the hot springs gully after the original bathhouse was badly damaged by a flood. *Alexander Turnbull Library.*

"No gardener should be let loose to work 'improvements'," he stipulated.[6] His superior, T. E. Donne, the Superintendent of the Tourist Department, agreed — "The chief charm of the place is a very pretty piece of bush".[7] His attitude was that it was easier for Napier people to get to Taupo's geothermal waters than those at Morere, and Gisborne, the other centre of population anywhere near Morere, would be better served by Te Puia Hot Springs.

The department complied with the petition to the extent of building a small bathhouse in 1904. It was lit by natural gas collected from the springs. The overflow from the bathhouse ran into an open air bath and further down the valley there was a spring of sulphuretted drinking water.

The bathhouse was partly washed away by a flood in 1910. While experiments were carried out to pipe the water further down the valley, the damaged bath-house was propped up so that people could use it. Another storm washed away some of the pipeline in 1911 and half-filled the baths with silt.

Morere bathers had to make do with the propped up bathhouse until 1918 when another was erected further down the valley. The site of the original house was reconstructed into a large swimming pool, but the Wairoa Chamber of Commerce was not happy with some of the arrangements. It wrote in 1918:

> Persons undressing have to hang their clothes up in the steamy atmosphere . . . there is no proper circulation of the water supply, the pipes carrying the hot water flowing in at the top and the overflow running out at the same level. This practically means that the bulk of the water in the baths is not disturbed except by persons displacing same when bathing, which from a health point of view is very undesirable, especially as these baths are used by Maoris as well as Europeans.[8]

This followed an earlier complaint that, during the period 1895–1900, Europeans wishing to have a bath used to grow so impatient with Maoris occupying the pools that wrestling matches would take place for possession of the best bathing holes.

A women's bathhouse containing 2 tiled baths was constructed in 1919, but there was criticism about lack of supervision. A Wellington man wrote in February 1921: "I found this place open and being used by men. It was open and the first Maori dropping in off the road".[9]

The Government appointed a caretaker, a Mr E. J. Kennedy, who then looked after the reserve and the bathhouses for 25 years. Initially he had to live in a tent for some months until the weather drove him into the hotel. One of his tasks was to hand out lamps to tourists finding their way up the valley to the baths at night. From 1919 until 1936 visitors to Morere had a choice of the No. 1 bathhouse, for women, the No. 2 bathhouse with its 3 baths or the large bath.

It was in 1924 that the second major problem with Morere springs became evident: the comparatively small flow of the springs. Leakages from the wooden stave pipes carrying water from the springs to the baths magnified the problem. During that year the women's bathhouse could not be used because of lack of water and only 1 of the 3 baths in the middle bathhouse was usable.

Morere was the first geothermal water area to introduce mixed bathing — with costumes — in the large pool near the top of the gully. This proved very popular and was also introduced at Rotorua's Blue Baths. Unfortunately, Morere did not provide sufficient dressing accommodation and the Wairoa Chamber of Commerce again expressed its concern: "privacy is reported as almost impossible. Considering that both sexes use the bath you can imagine the state of affairs".[10] The *Gisborne Times*, too, had something to say on the subject, claiming on 14 April 1928 that "the two cubicles abutting the bath itself have a piece of mildewed calico curtaining the doorway. Many a thrill was occasioned when this curtain was drawn aside by one (sometimes of the opposite sex) in search of a dressing crib".[11]

Another flood in 1929 knocked in the side wall of the top bathhouse and filled the bath with shingle, rocks and earth. For several years the women's bathhouse had to be closed during winter so that there was sufficient water for the middle bath.

So that both sexes could use this middle bathhouse, a complicated arrangement of open and locked doors was suggested, but the caretaker thought this would "make it easy for the peeping Tom type, which have given a good deal of trouble in the past and to a person of this type the doors would afford him a good opportunity of spying on lady bathers".[12] He suggested that the small baths, known as the coffin baths, be converted into a single bath for women only. In this way the middle baths could be used by both men and women, and peeping Toms would be thwarted.

The springs' small outflow and their distance from the bottom of the valley made the next development difficult. For some time it had been suggested that a proper swimming pool was needed near the entrance to the reserve. The pool,

The swimming pool shown in this 1950 photograph was constructed in 1936. The supply of hot water from the springs above the bath was a problem through the 1960s. Since then Morere's bathhouses have been redeveloped. *Alexander Turnbull Library.*

completed in March 1936, is the one usually shown in postcards of Morere.

Part of the reserve had to be closed in 1953 as a flood washed both path and pipeline away. Similarly, in 1960, the top bath was unusable for much of the year because of landslip damage. The social problem hadn't disappeared, either. "Much damage has been done," it was reported in 1962, "by 'Peeping Toms' drilling holes in the partition walls in both No. 1 and No. 2 buildings".[13]

Because of the danger of falling rocks, the No. 3 bathhouse at the top of the gully was abandoned and a large new indoor public pool was opened in 1963 on the flat area beneath the bush reserve. The smaller 1936 swimming pool is now a cold swimming bath. The old bathhouses have disappeared but the new Nikau Bath occupies the site of the lowest one. There are 2 more private pools.

When the Tourist Department withdrew from geothermal spa interests, the Morere Hot Springs Reserve reverted to normal Crown Land Reserve status in 1971. It is now, under the care of the Lands and Survey Department, becoming better known for its botanical resources. There are 200 ha of rimu, matai, totara, kohekohe and tawa, and the reserve is famous for its nikau palm groves.

References

1   *Appendices to the Journal of the House of Representatives*, 1897, c-1.
2   *Ibid.*, 1901, c-1.
3   James Cooper, Hot Springs Hotel, Morere, to the Hon. James Carroll, Member of the House of Representatives, 3 September 1901. Tourist Department file 1901/101.
4   M. J. Joblin, Chairman, Nuhaka Settlers' Association, to Sir Joseph Ward, Minister for Tourist and Health Resorts, September 1901. Tourist Department file 1901/101.
5   Petitioners from Gisborne, Cook and Wairoa Counties and visitors to Morere Hot Springs, to the Premier and Members of Cabinet, April 1903.
6   A. S. Wohlmann, Government Balneologist, to T. E. Donne, Superintendent, Department of Tourist and Health Resorts, 8 September 1902.
7   T. E. Donne, Superintendent, to Minister for Tourist and Health Resorts, 18 August 1903.
8   A. W. Lockhart, Wairoa Chamber of Commerce, to Minister of Tourist and Health Resorts, 10 October 1918.
9   Stanley Muir to Minister of Tourist Resorts, 4 February 1921.
10 W. Hamilton Irvine, Hon. Secretary, Gisborne Chamber of Commerce, to General Manager, Tourist Resorts, 24 April 1928.
11 *Gisborne Times*, 14 April 1928.
12 E. J. Kennedy, Caretaker, Government Baths, Morere, to Manager, Tourist Department, 6 February 1932.
13 Reserves Manager, Morere, to General Manager, Department of Tourist and Publicity, 9 June 1962.

16 Te Puia

There has been a pleasant, comfortable hotel at Te Puia's hot springs, north of Gisborne, since 1934. Before 1929, however, when the first section of the hotel opened, visitors to this attractive area had to endure the most primitive of conditions.

Although the Department of Tourist and Health Resorts concentrated most of its spending on Rotorua, Hanmer and Te Aroha, it recognised that other potentially valuable hot springs areas could be linked into a chain of scenic tourist attractions. But reasonable roading and accommodation were needed to make isolated areas, such as Te Puia, Morere or Maruia, appealing to travellers, especially in view of the slowness and discomfort of coach transport.

Te Puia Hot Springs Hotel, about 1935. *Alexander Turnbull Library.*

The accommodation house at Te Puia Springs, 1901. It burned down in November 1918 and for several years there was no accommodation at the springs. *National Archives.*

Unfortunately, however, there was not enough money to provide good roading for many attractive but remote places such as Te Puia — and not enough people in the district to press the Government for such improvements. When a lack of accommodation was combined with roads usable only in summer, the resulting trickle of visitors would not inspire the Government to put money into the region. Te Puia, like Maruia Springs in the South Island, was a victim of this kind of vicious circle. Although Te Puia was, to some extent, cut off during the winter, sub-standard accommodation was the area's worst problem.

The first accommodation at Te Puia appeared when Mr David Gordon built a hut and roofed 2 bathhouses. He leased 0.4 ha from the Lands and Survey Department, partly through the assistance of the Waiapu MP James Carroll. In a 1902 letter to Tourist and Health Resorts Superintendent Thomas Donne, Gordon explained that when "Mr Carroll and Mr Percy Smith, late Surveyor General, were here they put me in charge of the springs. Mr Carroll asked me not to 'push' the Government too much". Gordon added, "I will see that everything is done as well and as cheap as possible".[1] The nearby Waiapu County Council described the Te Puia accommodation as being "constructed from packing cases".[2]

Henry J. Matthews, the Chief Forester for the Tourist Department, was the first to inspect and report on Te Puia. He also covered the difficulties of journeying to the springs: "The Steamer 'Omapere' leaves Gisborne fortnightly, calling at all bays on the East Coast, and returns from Auckland about a week later. Leaving

Gisborne at noon, Waipiro Bay [the nearest harbour to Te Puia Springs] is reached about 8 a.m. the following day. Landing is effected by the Ship's boats towed by an oil launch, and passengers and cargo are trans-shipped into a wagon among the breakers". He then described the land approach: "From Waipiro to Te Puia it is quite impossible to keep to the road . . . A coach runs from Gisborne to Tolaga Bay, bi-weekly, the remainder of the journey [thirty-five miles] having to be done on horseback, owing to the bad state of the roads." He went on to mention Gordons' improvements: 2 bathhouses with timber-lined baths. "Ventilation on the top is urgently required as the presence of vapour during dull weather necessitates bathing with the door open, which is neither comfortable nor agreeable."[3]

Even at this stage, 1902, one of the bathhouses was lit by a pipe sunk into the ground to concentrate the emission of methane gas. Te Puia was one of three New Zealand thermal bathing areas (the others were Hanmer and Morere) to use natural gas for lighting and heating. The 1.2 m flame from the pipe could be seen at night by passing steamers.

Gordon had built both bathhouses at his own expense and had, by the time of Matthews' report, accommodation for 15 people, with more construction in progress. The Forester's comment was: "The present accommodation is barely equal to a third-rate boarding house. The beds are clean, but the rooms have a most disagreeable odour through want of air and sunlight."[4] The charges were 1 shilling and sixpence per meal and the same amount per bed.

Suddenly, on 13 December 1902, Mrs Gordon was presented with a telegram, through the Napier office of the Lands and Survey Department: "Government decided to terminate accommodation house lease — what amounts do you require as compensation for surrender, taking into consideration your appointment as caretaker?"[5] Mrs Gordon pointed out that they had been caretakers for 3 years, but not paid as such, that they had borrowed money to provide more accommodation and that a son had "left a good billet in Gisborne to help with the work".[6] The Lands and Survey Department suggested a compensation of £723 (including £35 for the 2 bathhouses), adding that it had no funds to pay this sum. The letter from the Under-Secretary asks whether the Tourist Department will find the necessary "moneys" to pay the compensation.[7]

By April 1904 the Gordons had still not been paid £35 for the original bathhouses and were reluctant to do any more building. In another letter, on 15 July, Mrs Gordon explained that her husband's illness was adding to their difficulties. (Mr Gordon had been ruptured while lifting a crippled invalid from a bath.)

The completion of the accommodation house resulted in a coaching service being extended to the springs. This immediately increased the numbers of visitors: a 1904 Lands Department report recorded that on Sundays up to 20 people called at the accommodation house for a meal and a bath.

Mrs Gordon's problems were helped only slightly by finally receiving the £35 for the 2 bathhouses — her husband had been an invalid for 2 years. She desperately hoped that some Government department would act upon the Commissioner's recommendation for assuming the lease and compensate her.

Te Puia Springs, 1906. This is one of 2 small bathhouses; 1 was used by European visitors, the other by the Ngati Porou people of the area. *National Archives*.

As a result of Mrs Gordon writing to the Premier, Richard John Seddon, in 1905, he found that the Commissioner of Crown Lands in Napier was not empowered by the Tourist Department to negotiate for the termination of the lease. The Gordons seem to have been the victims of a lack of communication between 2 departments.

The Te Puia springs were still very isolated in the early years of the twentieth century. Wohlmann, the Government Balneologist, tried twice to visit the area but was stopped both times by bad weather and the condition of the roads. His planned investigation had been prompted by a request from the Poverty Bay Farmers Union for the Government to take over the Te Puia Springs. The union insisted that the accommodation was totally inadequate.

When the doctor *did* manage to get to Te Puia on his third attempt, in May of 1906, his report was optimistic: "I may say at once that I was favourably impressed with the potentialities of the place, and that, while the present traffic alone would constitute it a profitable business concern, the excellence of the waters and the picturesque site afford a sufficient inducement for the Government to buy the place." He suggested the place was suitable for a sanatorium, "being on a hillside with extensive views over the sea and surrounding country".[8] The hill was known to the Ngati Porou people as Pahuri-tane-nui. Near it was a large natural pool which had been used as the local wai-ariki or bathing pool for centuries before the bathhouses were built. From the nineteenth century it was called Hiroama, from the biblical pool of Siloam.

Access had improved by this time; a coach was running twice a week, to and from Gisborne to Waipiro Bay, right through the year. Two ships called regularly at Waipiro Bay — the Union Steamship Company's *Haupiri* and the Farmers Union ship *Kotara*.

Wohlmann gave credit to the Gordons for their work: "The accommodation house is on an excellent site, but is rough and unfinished, some of the walls being still merely sacking. Considering, however, the immense difficulties under which the Gordons built the place it is surprisingly comfortable . . . In addition to the ramshackle original cottage there are eight bedrooms, one sitting room and one dining room, giving accommodation for 12 boarders."

There was a large bath, kept locked and reserved for visitors, and a small bath, "open to the Maoris of the district". He added: "The bathing accommodation is primitive and totally inadequate. No separate provision is made for ladies, or for persons suffering from infectious complaints."[9]

The Waiapu County Council's hospital, being built a short distance away, would mean that medical aid and advice were at hand. Wohlmann also thought that the natural gas should be used for fuel and lighting, that the Government should purchase the Gordon's interest in the accommodation house, and that both the house and the baths should be extended.

In August 1906, however, Mr Gordon was still unwell and Mrs Gordon was still waiting for settlement so as to get him medical treatment. The couple eventually accepted an offer of £700 in April 1907 and received their money 3 months later.

The Government had taken over a very Spartan house. In the unfinished new section the ceiling of the dining room was "only covered with cretonne, while part of the sitting-room ceiling is not covered at all". There were no skirting boards; the old portion was built from boxes and split timber; the floor of the old dining room was whitewashed clay. In the kitchen, one of the stoves was useless "on account of the side being burnt out".[10] At the same time more bathing facilities were provided by diverting the overflow of a spring into a depression and creating an earth-surrounded swimming pool.

The greater Government involvement meant that Te Puia was mentioned, briefly, in 1907 for the first time in a Parliamentary report, by the Public Works Department: "When they [the springs] are better known, good access, and better accommodation provided, I feel sure that the place will become a favourite health resort."[11]

From 1901 various authorities prophesied a good future for Te Puia but no one provided the money to make it possible. Curiously, though, the Government bought the small township of Te Puia from the Tairawhiti Maori Board in 1911, for just over £3,000, partly because of a probable commitment to a proper accommodation house.

During the prolonged negotiations for the sale there had been a particularly sad chapter in Te Puia's history. The caretakers who succeeded the Gordons were not a success and the Tourist Department ordered them out in August 1909. The department's inspector noted that "horses and stock have been allowed to have a free run around the house, the ground and paths being cut up like a cattle yard."[12]

The inspector had to wrestle with the caretaker to obtain the department's money, the man having drunk a considerable amount of whisky during the inspection. The couple's children were packed off in a coach and the wife set off to walk to Tokomaru Bay, until the inspector provided her with a horse. The caretaker then sobered up. Stock on the Government reserve had to be sold off for next to nothing; some of the beasts could hardly move because of lack of feed.

The third pair of caretakers, Mr and Mrs G. W. Good, tried to improve conditions by dismantling the original house behind the tourist quarters; Mr Good found there was only enough wood to build a wash house. The original building, which had accommodated the occasional traveller between 1898 and 1902, had been constructed on a framework of manuka poles and 1 end was covered by sacks. The squalor of deep mud in the drive up to the house and the cow pats around the bathhouses with their peeling weatherboards hardly created the conditions expected at a tourist centre.

The Government never intended to establish an international spa at Te Puia, but with better roads and accommodation it could have been a more important tourist node, along with Morere Hot Springs and the Government development at Waikaremoana.

The Goods did what they could with limited resources. Because women objected to the lack of privacy in the bathhouse that had lost its weatherboards, it was rebuilt to half its original size so it could be covered with what timber remained. The Goods managed to improve the area around the bathhouses by erecting a galvanised iron fence to keep cattle out.

The accommodation house, however, had to be rebuilt. During wet weather there was not a single dry room in the house, and an inspection in November 1913 revealed that there was "an excessive mustiness in the bedrooms, rendering them almost repulsive to visitors on first entering".[13] The *Poverty Bay Herald* in January 1914 described the Te Puia buildings as a "collection of ramshackle shanties".[14]

By now G. W. Good was suffering real hardship. He wrote in March 1914 to tell the department that, with the failure of the gas supply, he couldn't afford coal and wood. Fencing was "flat on the ground". He had had only 1 guest in the last fortnight, and added "I am about at the end of my funds".[15] He wrote again in May to say that a downpour had washed much of the paper off 1 passage wall, and that some of the beds were soaking wet. "It was very fortunate", he added, "that there were only two men in the house." He sent, "under separate cover", some of the washed-off wallpaper.[16] The situation was no better by February 1915: "People will not come to the place in its present state, it is simply disgraceful. I am quite ashamed of it . . . one end of the house has settled down so that the water will not run towards the tanks [which collected rainwater]." He felt the outlook was not very bright. What's more, the top of his good cooking range had cracked, and the crack widened every time he used it.[17]

In March the tank-stand with its 3 1800 litre tanks collapsed. Good asked for 5 kg of solder to repair the tanks. Two months later he took only £1 7s from visitors in 8 days and was down to his last bag of coal. The following month he told the department he was not going to accommodate women or children because there was no means of heating the sitting room. "I would not expect women or children to do without a fire at this season of the year," he explained, adding that the gas supply had again failed. The Government provided him with a subsidy of £100 on the condition that he kept the house open for another 2 months. He had asked to be relieved.[18]

By October 1 part of the building had separated from the other, leaving a gap of 10 cm. Without any fireplaces, everyone had to sit around the gas stove, and the fumes were too strong for some people. There was water on the floor and rain running down the walls. The Goods left in October and were replaced by the Cottrells, the lease being in the name of Mrs Constance Cottrell.

When the Public Works District Engineer for Gisborne reported in December that the house required some means of drying clothes (for guests getting wet going to and from the baths), that there were no baths or conveniences in the house, and that the path at the gate was knee deep in mud after the rain, the Tourist Department was unmoved: "There should be no need for provision to be made for the drying of wet clothes in the house as there is an abundance of room for clothes-lines outside."[19] It did, however, recommend that £100 be spent on urgent repairs. Several months later Mrs Cottrell insisted that something needed to be done about the paths around the house: "Visitors to this hotel go away on account of not being able to walk around after a day's rain".[20]

In 1916 there was, at last, some good news for Te Puia when the Government completed new baths in May, but the problems with the accommodation house continued. The General Manager of the Tourist Department again recommended a new building. The situation partly resolved itself when the hostel was destroyed by fire in November 1918, the day after the First World War ended. The Cottrells couldn't account for the blaze but, as caretakers for the baths, they urged the Government to rebuild without delay.

When Mrs Cottrell wrote in March 1919 she was cooking by means of a flame from a gas pipe, and in 1920 she told the General Manager that she hoped they would not have to endure another winter in the horse stable which, after the fire, was the only available accommodation.

Hopes rose near the end of 1922 when there was a suggestion that the Waipiro Bay Hotel be shifted to Te Puia, but a year later Mr Cottrell was still writing about the draughts in the stable. The department's attitude to the area was summed up by a statement from the General Manager in March of 1924: "Te Puia cannot be strictly called a tourist resort, and I do not think it will be for a good many years, being too far off the main routes."[21] In that year, however, the department did pay for the match-lining and the subdivision of the stable.

The public pool and spout bath at Te Puia developed by D. J. Barry, the firm which built the hotel. This pool was opened in January 1935. The photograph was taken in 1940. *Alexander Turnbull Library.*

By 1924 Te Puia was a 4-hour drive from Gisborne, instead of a 2-day coach journey, but the accommodation problem was not solved. The negotiation to have a hotel shifted from Waipiro Bay failed because of licensing laws. The idea finally perished when the hotel burned down in 1925.

The Waiapu County Council asked, in 1927, that as the Government was not prepared to spend large sums of money on the district, tenders be called for the leasing of the Hot Springs Reserve. The Tourist Department recommended that it go ahead, so tenders were called in March 1928 — and the tender included the putting up of a suitable accommodation house.

The long-awaited building, which was to end 20 years of ramshackle buildings, and 11 years (1918–29) of no accommodation, began in 1928. The following year the Cottrells left the stable, and their position as caretakers.

Development continued when the owner of the new accommodation house, J. R. Johnson, leased his interest in Te Puia Springs to D. J. Barry of Gisborne. Boxing Day of 1935 saw the opening of the present concrete swimming pool, a short distance behind the hotel. As well as transferring a licence to the accommodation house, Barry made considerable extensions and improvements. He landscaped the area about his Te Puia Hot Springs Hotel and built 2 small bathhouses, at a total cost of around £10,000. The improvement can be measured in the words of a 1941 Tourist Department letter: "The swimming baths and private baths controlled by Mr Barry are in excellent order and the hotel is very well run and can be safely recommended to visitors."[22] It is sad that a report such as that did not date from 1910.

Because the general public used the hotel swimming pool the Government baths fell into disuse in the 1950s. The building still stands as a skeleton among the springs and crags behind the hotel, a local symbol of the chain of small spas that existed in New Zealand from 1885 until the 1960s. The Tourist Department handed the reserve over to the Lands Department in 1971. Even private enterprise became less interested in the geothermal resource. The swimming bath was closed in 1981 and today only people staying at the modernised hotel can enjoy Te Puia spring water in a private pool.

The pathetic and sometimes almost unbelievable story of accommodation for bathers at Te Puia makes ironical reading of an 1883 *Auckland Weekly News* paragraph predicting a great future for Te Puia springs: "There is a capital opening for an enterprising person to institute baths and a decent accommodation house at the springs". The correspondent described them as "free to all, and accessible easily, and are of remarkable efficacy, the only drawback being the want of accommodation . . . — a want out of which any enterprising and energetic man can make a fortune."[23]

References

Unless otherwise indicated, all references for this chapter are to the T 0-1 files of the Tourist and Health Resorts Department.

1   D. Gordon to T. E. Donne, Superintendent, Department of Tourist and Health Resorts, 17 June 1902.
2   William Ryan, Clerk of Waiapu Council, to Surveyor-General, 30 September 1901.
3   H. J. Matthews, Chief Forester, to T. E. Donne, Superintendent, Department of Tourist and Health Resorts.
4   *Ibid.*
5   Eric C. Goldsmith, Commissioner, Crown Lands, Napier, to Jane Gordon, Te Puia.
6   Jane Gordon to Commissioner of Crown Lands, Napier, 13 December 1902.
7   Under Secretary, Department of Lands and Survey, to Superintendent, Department of Tourist and Health Resorts, 20 January 1904.
8   A. S. Wohlmann, Government Balneologist, to C. R. C. Robieson, Acting Superintendent of Department of Tourist and Health Resorts, 20 June 1906.
9   *Ibid.*
10   Frank Moorhouse, Inspector, to General Manager, Department of Tourist and Health Resorts, 22 July 1907.
11   *Appendices to the Journal of the House of Representatives*, 1907, H-31.
12   Frank Moorhouse, Inspector, to General Manager, Department of Tourist and Health Resorts, 18 August 1909.
13   Tourist Department memo, 1 November 1913.
14   *Poverty Bay Herald*, 26 January 1914.
15   G. W. Good to the Manager, Department of Tourist and Health Resorts, 3 March 1914.
16   G. W. Good to Manager, 20 May 1914.
17   G. W. Good to Manager, 8 February 1915.
18   G. W. Good to Manager, 10 June 1915.
19   Acting General Manager to Minister for Tourist and Health Resorts, 17 December 1915.
20   C. Cottrell to General Manager, 6 May 1916.
21   General Manager to Minister for Tourist and Health Resorts, 2 April 1924.
22   Assistant General Manager to General Manager, Department of Industries and Commerce, Tourist and Publicity, 24 March 1941.
23   *Auckland Weekly News*, 1883.

17 Awakeri

Bathers at the Awakeri hot springs could believe themselves to be a considerable distance from the rocks of the Volcanic Plateau, but in fact the same ignimbrite material underlies the alluvial lowland. To the south-west, along the same edge of the Raungaehe Range, are the bitter Waimangeao Soda Springs. Beneath the feet of Awakeri bathers was a considerable deposit of Tarawera ash — until the swimming pool was concreted in the 1960s.

The growth in Awakeri's popularity over the last 30 years parallels the development of nearby Whakatane as one of the country's most popular holiday and retirement centres. It is far enough away from Rotorua's geothermal resources to have become a hot water bathing area for the coast from Tauranga to Opotiki, as well as for the nearby population of Kawerau. The fact that the nearest hot spring areas at Onepu and Maketu are no longer used for bathing by the general public has greatly increased its use.

The Ngatiawa people of the Whakatane area called the springs Pukaahu and until the 1950s the Domain around the springs retained that name, although by Post Office decree the general locality lost its original label of Mangaroa early in the century. So Awakeri is a newly coined name, in the same way as Parakai.

Awakeri's hot springs were never high on the Department of Tourist and Health Resorts list of priorities for development. It was 6 years after his arrival as Government Balneologist that Dr Wohlmann finally made the short journey from Rotorua to look at the resources of the locality. At the time of his visit the vast Rangitaiki swamp was being drained; the springs were at one edge of this development.

The doctor described the nearby Te Teko hotel as being above average and the general area as certain to be a great tourist route in the near future. He found that the spring water was alkaline saline and commented that there was a very considerable flow from the main spring of over 100,000 gallons per day. He also noted that the 40 m long bathing pool was "without any accommodation whatever in the way of dressing boxes or screening".[1] He suggested 8 foot fencing around part of the pool to be used by women, while 5 feet 6 inches would be sufficient around the men's area. He also thought that digging out the Tarawera ash from the bottom of the pool would be an improvement. (This ash, of course, was from the 1886 eruption.)

In 1910 there was pressure from the Whakatane County Council for the Government to acquire the springs and vest them in the council. The Tourist

Awakeri Springs, c. 1908, before the bathing pool was developed. *Whakatane Museum.*

A 1920 photograph of Awakeri Springs. The bathing pool was boarded around its margins after a visit by the Government Balneologist. *Whakatane Museum.*

Department, however, advised the Government not to concern itself with Awakeri — especially as the springs of Rotorua were relatively close. The council tried a different tack in 1912, suggesting to the Government that the Awakeri hot springs area would make an excellent site for a hospital. (This was playing on the Government's current interest in spas.) Once again, however, the council's approach was unsuccessful, so a third attempt was made in 1914, with a different argument — "The natives are using the springs as a washing ground for their clothes and also bathe there and the europeans do not care to use the place in consequence, although a great number are very anxious to do so."[2]

The council pressure eventually had an effect and in 1919 the Government bought the Awakeri springs area from its Maori owners. A Hot Springs Domain Board was created the same year, but was not properly constituted until 1921. The board drew up regulations, including the requirement for neck to knee bathing costumes. It was difficult, however, for the board to police the area so control went to the Whakatane County Council in 1931. Nineteen years after its original approach to the Government, the council achieved its goal.

In the same year the council, too, found it hard to control the Hot Springs Domain and was concerned about "moonlight bathing parties, not too particular as to the necessity of bathing costumes".[3] The council suggested leasing the springs, pointing out that it regretted it could not finance the improvements needed. It was a situation common to many hot springs areas: the locals wanted their springs developed but nobody wanted to pay for it.

The policing of the springs obviously became a nightmare for the council, as a somewhat desperate 1932 letter to the Under Secretary for Lands indicated: "There is a very undesirable type, both Maori and Pakeha, which frequents the springs. The caretaker the Council established there last year had his tent burnt; was thrown into the Springs and told that 'if he didn't get out, he'd be done for'. He left the district and although an exhaustive police enquiry has been made, he has never since been found."[4] Quite apart from having his tent burnt and being thrown into the pool, the caretaker must have had a miserable existence living in a tent during the winter when frost lies even around the hot pool areas.

Apart from the debacle of the caretaker, though, the council had carried out useful work in draining all the swamp in the Domain and clearing out and deepening the pool. Finding someone prepared to lease and develop the Domain, however, proved to be very difficult. Originally offered in 1935, the council's proposition was not taken up until 1953.

The Awakeri Springs resort popular as a holiday place today owes its development largely to Mr V. H. McChesney. He drained the hollow which had served as a bath for 50 years and in 1968 replaced it with a concrete pool. Along with dressing rooms, he provided the locality with shops, tearooms and recreational facilities. His successors have added private spa pools, their water drawn from bores. The neat modern surroundings of Awakeri Hot Springs are a contrast to the scrub and ash-floored pool of the old Pukaahu Reserve. The place has become one of the success stories of recreational use of a relatively small hot springs area.

Awakeri in 1954. The popular holiday camp built up around these springs was mainly the work of Mr V. McChesney, in the 1950s and 1960s. The main spring is the fenced-in area immediately under the hill. *Hisken's Airviews, courtesy Mr G. Timbs.*

References

1   Government Balneologist to General Manager, Department of Tourist and Health Resorts, 19 August 1908. Tourist Department file 1908/314.
2   Whakatane County Council to Director, Department of Agriculture, Commerce and Tourists, 17 March 1914. Tourist Department file 1910/153.
3   Whakatane County Council to Under Secretary of Lands, 28 May 1931. Lands and Survey file 611, Tourist Department file 20/47.
4   Whakatane County Council to Under Secretary of Lands, 1932.

18 Okoroire

The hot springs which lie outside the Volcanic Plateau are often found in more attractive settings. The Okoroire Springs, at the extreme south of the Waikato, are a case in point, with their avenues of old plane trees and a hotel overlooking the Waihou River. There is an unusual waterfall and enormous macrocarpas form an almost Gothic vaulting over the path to the bathhouses.

For some people, one of the delightful aspects of Okoroire is that it has remained largely unchanged since it first advertised itself as a spa in 1889. Part of the original hotel burned in 1915 but the replacement was in a similar style to the original. Similarly, there has been very little alteration to the bathhouses. One half expects to pass someone in Edwardian costume on the way to the springs.

The Okoroire Springs began to attract Europeans in 1883, when the road from Tirau to Rotorua was completed, but the springs were already well known to the Ngati Raukawa, whose carved house Tokopikowhakahau stood only 3 km away.

Hayr's guide described Okoroire in 1888 as an estate of 29 ha "on which there are rapids, cascades and waterfalls",[1] and claimed that the medicinal properties of these springs were the equal of any in the lake district, that is, around Rotorua. No authority was given for this statement; no analysis of the spring water was included. The assertion was typical of many such late nineteenth-century publications. The statement, "It is without doubt the finest water in the country", is found, with variations, in much tourist literature of the 1880s and 1890s. Hayr's guide, without having measured the flow of Okoroire, claimed blithely that the springs were "capable of supplying hundreds of baths with a continual supply".[2] Similarly, there were "marvellous cures of gout, rheumatism, lumbago, sciatica, affection of the eyes.".

L. D. Nathan and Company built the Okoroire hotel during the summer of 1888–89. Apart from its position overlooking the river (a good trout stream) and its closeness to the springs, the hotel was only a short distance from a station on the uncompleted Auckland–Rotorua railway. The company took advantage of the fact that the railhead was some distance from Rotorua. It offered a comfortable hotel 50 km from the town, and a scenic coach drive to its Geyser Hotel at Whakarewarewa. As in the 1890s it was a 10-hour trip from Auckland to the railhead at Tarukenga, many passengers were pleased to alight at Okoroire.

In 1893 the *New Zealand Graphic* published an article on Okoroire, as part of a series entitled *Health and Pleasure Resorts of New Zealand*. The article suggested that Okoroire, "though perhaps the last discovered", would "always occupy a promi-

Okoroire photographed in about 1890. Many travellers to this tiny spa claimed that the landscape reminded them of the Scottish Highlands. The Fairy Bath was to the left of the 3 bathhouses. *Photograph by George Valentine. Rotorua Museum.*

nent position in the first rank of New Zealand's health and pleasure resorts".[3] In fact, many South Islanders have never heard of Okoroire, just as many North Islanders have never head of Maruia Springs on the Lewis Pass Road. The *Graphic* suggested that a stop at Okoroire was the best way to break "the weary, dreary journey" to the "Hot Lakes",[4] a long haul made tedious by "incontinently long waits" at many stations. So many passengers made the stop at Okoroire that an extra building had to be added to the hotel.

Journalists at this time did not lack confidence in their own powers of discernment or in their sources of information — "The Baths of Okoroire are usually spoken of as the best appointed in the colony."[5] Had the writer for the *Graphic* inspected bathhouses at Hanmer, Te Aroha, Rotorua or Waiwera? Too frequently, articles were advertisements rather than examples of objective journalism.

The small No. 1 bathhouse is the only one of the original bathhouses that no longer exists. It was "erected for the convenience of those unfortunates whose ailments make it undesirable that they should patronise the public baths." In the No. 2 bathhouse the "scrupulous cleanliness of the concrete, which is free of any deposit [Okoroire water has little silica or sulphur] invariably attracts the commendatory attention of the visitors."[6] An 1894 advertisement, too, emphasised that the Okoroire Springs were free from any unpleasant odour or deposit, a fact

As this 1895 photograph shows, the Fairy Bath at Okoroire is one of the most attractive bathing pools in the country. *Photograph by Josiah Martin, Rotorua Museum.*

which was supposed to make them especially attractive to people in good health. The advertisement was also, of course, pointed against Rotorua's hydrogen sulphide.

Originally, the River Bath had a 2.7 m spout of hot water similar to that of the Spout Bath at Whakarewarewa. The name originated from the fact that a covered way led to a bay of the Waihou River. Bathers could achieve a sauna effect by moving from the hot bath into the cold water of the river. This feature has been removed because it was extremely dangerous. If any swimmer were caught in the main current, he or she most likely would be carried over the falls and, as the *Graphic* put it, "the most powerful adept at natation would have a poor chance".[7]

Okoroire is probably best known for the Fairy Bath or, as it was often called, the Glow Worm Bath, set in a fern-covered basin. Gas bubbles rise from the gravel bottom of this natural pool, but as there is no roof, there is no problem of gas build up. Today's electric lights mean that the glow worm display is now not so brilliant, but otherwise this bath is still as attractive as it was in the 1890s.

The hotel also had the advantage of hosts who were "indefatigable in assisting guests to accomplish excursions". The *Graphic* reported that the hotel manager and his wife "throw themselves into the spirit of the thing . . ."[8] Certainly, this reach of the Waihou River and the nearby Waimakariri Stream offer picturesque localities for picnics and fishing trips.

Two important photographers were responsible for 2 brochures advertising Okoroire. In the *Guide for Tourists En Route for Rotorua*, published about 1891, the photographs were taken by George Valentine. He came to New Zealand in the 1880s with the hope that the climate would help combat his tuberculosis. He died in the 1890s, after taking the most impressive of all the photographs of the Volcanic Plateau. In 1898 Valentine's father's firm in Dundee published a magnificent brochure with illustrations by the Auckland photographer, Josiah Martin. As an amateur geologist, Martin was particularly interested in hot springs.

The brochures were designed to attract the sportsman as well as the invalid. The virtues of trout fishing and pheasant shooting in this area were extolled. Many visitors, apparently, found that the countryside around Okoroire reminded them of the grouse shooting areas of Scotland.

Lawn tennis and croquet were provided and small detached departments were built for invalids. Apart from lack of medical supervision, travellers who had visited European spas no doubt recognised Okoroire as being a like institution. Cook's guide in 1901 described Okoroire as being unequalled as a health resort,[9] a statement that must have irritated the Government after it had spent £30,000 on the Rotorua spa between 1881 and 1901. (*The New Zealand Official Handbook* of 1892 made no mention of Okoroire in the section *Route to Rotorua*.)

The material on Okoroire in the fifth edition of Cook's guide in 1905 was written by Thomas Hope Lewis who, 20 years earlier, had been the first Medical Officer associated with geothermal bathing at Rotorua. Dr Hope Lewis claimed that there were 2 distinct waters at Okoroire: one was rich in iron and the other sulphurous. He also praised the bracing climate of the place. Some of the famous hydropathic centres in Europe were in bleak locations, areas that most certainly had "bracing climates". Dr Hope Lewis was familiar with at least the British examples.

After 1905 most tourist literature was published by the Tourist and Health Resorts Department, and because Okoroire was a geographical rival of a department spa that was losing money, it was mentioned only once in Government publications: "Certainly at Okoroire one meets with hot springs and other thermal action, but they are small compared to those in Rotorua".[10]

Okoroire's decline in significance was partly a result of technology. In 1907, when new engines were introduced to the Auckland-Rotorua railway, the time taken on the journey was cut down to 7½ hours. People continued on to Rotorua and Okoroire lost its advantage.

References

11 *Hayr's Tourist Guide to the Hot Lakes of New Zealand . . .*, Auckland, Scott, 1888.
2 *Ibid.*
3 "Okoroire" from the series "Health and Pleasure Resorts of New Zealand" in the *New Zealand Graphic*, 1893.
4-8 *Ibid.*
9 *The Wonderland of the World, New Zealand as a tourist and health resort*, Thomas Cook, 1901.
10 *The New Zealand Official Yearbook 1910*, Government Printer, 1910.

19 Okauia

Most New Zealanders have not heard of Okauia Springs, the correct name for the springs 7 km from Matamata. The groups of springs on either bank of the Waihou River had specific names which have fallen out of use. Undoubtedly at least 1 of the 3 groups of springs was used by the great chief, Wiremu Tamihana, from the nearby Okauia pa of Peria. Before him, Te Waharoa probably bathed in the spring called Ramaroa, and so back through generations of the Ngati Haua people.

The Waihou River runs parallel to the fault line also associated with hot springs at Okoroire and Te Aroha, and the mineral springs at Puriri and Paeroa.

There is comparatively little literature about the Okauia Springs. The Government showed no interest after learning that the water did not possess any unique qualities. Nor did either group of springs have nearby Okoroire's advantage of a powerful firm, L. D. Nathan and Company, to finance magnificent brochures.

The most significant spring of either group, Ramaroa, was used for medicinal bathing by the Ngati Haua, according to *Brett's Almanac* of 1880. It is now the private pool at Opal Springs. The *Almanac* described its idyllic setting at the bottom of a fern-covered cliff, close to the Waihou River:

> The hot water rises in a rocky oval basin about 20 feet long by 8 feet wide. The water rises round an old tree stump which projects from the bed of the water, which is 2 feet deep with a sandy bottom. On 3 sides of the basin the banks rise abruptly to a height of 30 feet and are profusely covered with verdure of every hue and variety. This hot spring is a charming spot, sheltered from all winds, and after reclining in the hot water, a plunge into the river is an invigorating finale. The spring has for ages been famed among the natives for its healing virtues. In cases of rheumatism it has worked the most surprising cures.[1]

When the intended Auckland–Rotorua railway line reached Matamata in 1886, Wilson and Horton published what is now a very rare paper, *Matamata: Its Hot Springs and Scenery*. Much of this reprint from a *Herald* article was devoted to the work of J. C. Firth, the pioneer farmer in this south-east corner of the Waikato. The Matamata Springs were on his 16 160 ha block.

Although Firth did a great deal to make the Waihou navigable, it was very difficult for river steamers to get upstream as far as Matamata. Only the railway made it worthwhile to advertise the springs — and the fact that, in 1886, nearby Te Aroha was the most important spa in the country.

Matamata's Opal Springs, c. 1930. *Cleaver family, Opal Hot Springs.*

The pamphlet explained that Mr Firth had "thrown open the spring [Ramaroa] to all comers".[2] Allowing people simply to use the spring was not enough, however; there was nowhere for tourists or invalids to stay. Two years later L. D. Nathan and Company erected a comfortable hotel next to the Okoroire Springs (only 20 km from Matamata). It is doubtful whether the Auckland firm would have done so had good accommodation been available at Okauia. As it was, the hotel at Okoroire tended to siphon off a considerable proportion of the travellers on their way to the Hot Lakes District and so Matamata did not become part of the tourist circuit. A vicious circle developed: because only a small number of bathers visited Matamata during the years from 1880 to 1920 it wasn't worth building an accommodation house at Okauia. Until there was an increase in population in the Waikato area, Okoroire choked Okauia's development.

Some developments had been made at Ramaroa, although it was such an attractive spring that it may have been better to have left it as natural as possible. The pamphlet described the alterations. "Mr Firth has close-boarded the small ravine from which this grand spring gushes. The side facing the river is closed by a high concrete wall. Passing along a concrete platform, on the river side of which runs a low balustrade, we enter a Gothic doorway . . ."[3] There were concrete dressing rooms, in front of which was a concrete platform and steps down to the bath.

The water apparently passed through the Ramaroa bath so rapidly that "Were a dozen of the dirtiest or most diseased persons to bathe in this grand bath, so great is its volume that ten minutes after, the most fastidious could dip into its pellucid waters without fear of taint." Ramaroa was highly recommended: "Too many of us, we fear, have too often 'bad quarters of an hour', but that fifteen

The Crystal Springs in about 1920. The pool was formed by damming the flow of several springs in a gully. The original name for the springs was Papahuia. *Alexander Turnbull Library.*

minutes spent in the Opal Fountain will forever shine in our calendar as 'a good quarter of an hour'."[4] (The name derived from the pale blue colour of the water.)

Across the river was Papahuia, the other main group of springs near Matamata. In 1886 they were known as the Diamond Springs, but for most of this century they have been called the Crystal Springs, because small crystals, that looked like diamonds, could be found in them. One hundred years ago their setting was a swamp gully, and the overflow of several springs formed a stream that drained into the Waihou.

The pamphlet made suggestions as to how J. C. Firth should develop the area as a spa. More springs were required for the recuperation of patients and the amusement of friends. A township was needed, along with various recreational amenities. One idea was to fill in a depression so that convalescents could enjoy boating; for the healthy section of the community, winding carriage drives through "rocky and rugged ravines"[5] were recommended. While many of these proposals were 15 years ahead of developments at Rotorua, Te Aroha and Hanmer, the extent of the undertaking very likely had the effect of causing Firth to concentrate on agriculture.

Various members of the Firth family offered the springs to the Government in 1902 and the Balneologist examined the area in 1903. One paragraph of Wohlmann's report probably killed Government interest in Matamata:

> The Matamata waters then are of a very weak alkaline saline nature. While not without medicinal value their properties would be so feeble as compared with the many excellent and better-known springs of the same class that I do not think they will ever be very much used for therapeutic purposes. There is no doubt, however, that they would make an excellent and palatable table water.[6]

This 1955 photograph of the Crystal Springs shows the swimming pool which was last used in 1971. The Crystal Springs became Moana Iti, with an indoor pool. *Alexander Turnbull Library.*

The Opal Springs in the 1950s. *Alexander Turnbull Library.*

So Matamata was left to private developers and the Crystal Springs were the first to be modified for bathing, in 1905. The principal owner (in a syndicate) was Mr G. J. Garland, an Auckland land agent. For many years the springs on the right bank of the Waihou were known as Garland's Hot Springs. The stream in the gully was dammed in 1905 to create a bathing pool. For several years the stream flowed through the pool, creating an effect similar to the stream baths at Wairakei.

Both Crystal Springs and Opal Springs became very popular with their sizeable outdoor swimming pools, 36 x 9 m and 18 x 7 m respectively. The Crystal Springs bath, now no longer used, was in an attractive gully surrounded by native trees. It closed down as a public resort at the end of 1971, reopened in 1976 as Moana Iti, with a large indoor pool, but has since closed again. Opal Springs, with the Ramaroa Spring as its private pool, is one of the most popular geothermal bathing centres in the country.

Because the Department of Tourist and Health Resorts was not interested in the area for medicinal purposes, the 2 main groups of springs at Okauia were among the first to be developed almost entirely for recreation, often with associated camping, holiday visits and picnics. The large bath at Crystal Springs was 1 of only 2 geothermal baths with a high diving board, but since the discovery of amoebic meningitis in this country in 1969, such active use of untreated geothermal water has ceased. The pools of the 1980s are often indoor, usually fed by bores or by heat exchange.

References

1   *Brett's Almanac*, 1880.
2   *Matamata: its hot springs and scenery*, Auckland, Wilson & Horton, 1886.
3   *Ibid.*
4   *Ibid.*
5   *Ibid.*
6   A. S. Wohlmann, Government Balneologist, to Minister for Tourist and Health Resorts, 2 May 1903. Tourist Department file 1902/155.

20 Parakai

Helensville residents watching the development of the nearby Parakai Springs early this century must have felt as though they were following a tennis match. For years the Helensville Domain Board sent requests to the Government, and for years the Government ducked the requests or partly satisfied them. Usually Parakai got what it needed 2 or 3 years after it asked for it, and requests and reports went back and forth between Helensville and Wellington.

Like several other hot springs in New Zealand, Parakai would have been a more successful spa had it been developed by 1900 rather than 1930. When people were enthusiastic about "taking the cure" the Parakai bath was housed in a hut in a treeless paddock. When the area was complete with croquet pavilions, masseurs and adequate bathing facilities, New Zealanders' enthusiasm for the waters was waning, the Depression had almost stopped travel and the attractive little spa deteriorated.

Nineteenth-century travellers do not seem to have recorded their reactions to the waters of this area, which has only been known as Parakai since the 1890s. There was only 1 natural hot pool, although other springs rose through a creek bed. Apart from the people in the immediate locality, the general public's attention was first drawn to the area by the *Auckland Star* in 1902. "This spring," it claimed, "has been proved by experts to possess equally as good healing properties as are possessed at our existing sanatoriums."[1] (Perhaps the Edwardians were less sceptical than the generations of a more technological culture; readers of the last few decades would probably have asked, "Which experts? And with what evidence?") The article proposed a small sanatorium.

Because of Parakai's proximity to Auckland the Tourist Department's Superintendent ordered a report on the prospects of the place. He was told: "There is at present only one good spring . . . enclosed by a straggling building of a nondescript character."[2] There were 4 baths. Both hot and cold water had to be pumped by hand. According to the article, a peculiarity of the area was that the water was very hot in winter but "scarcely more than tepid" in summer. An analysis by J. A. Pond demonstrated that the spring water was not merely hot salt water (Parakai is very close to the Kaipara harbour).

The area had been gazetted as a recreation reserve, in 1883, when William Rolleston was Minister of Lands, and from 1902 the Domain Board lobbied the Tourist Department to take over the hot springs. The Superintendent suggested "that amounts aggregate to £1000 be placed on the Estimates for the purpose of

Parakai's 1910 swimming bath. Until 1924 men and women took turns to use the bath. At this stage the development of Parakai was championed by MP Gordon Coates. *Auckland Public Library Photograph Collection.*

building pleasure baths". He emphasised "pleasure baths" because of the expense involved in "medicinal baths". He added, for Parliament's benefit, that "these springs do not possess any particular medicinal value distinct from other mineral waters in the Province".[3] Parliament, of course, thought of Rotorua when hot water was mentioned, and any place requesting money for geothermal bathing had to demonstrate either something different from Rotorua, and valuable, or a remoteness from already developed bath areas.

The Helensville Domain Board's 1905 statement of income and expenditure at Parakai showed why it could not replace the "nondescript" bathhouse. Income amounted to £68 19s 3d; "wages of caretaker, repairing fences etc."[4] cost the board over £74. As a result of the inadequate facilities, many people who travelled from Auckland to Parakai on a day trip, went home again without having had a bath. A Helensville petition to Parliament in the same year explained that the Parakai baths would "become an untold benefit to the working people of Auckland and surrounding districts" if £1,000 were spent on them.[5]

Between 1902 and 1910 the Government Balneologist visited every significant group of hot springs in the country, and he was sent to Parakai as part of one of his expeditions. With a rail link to Helensville, his journey, in 1906, was easy, compared with the extraordinary difficulty Dr Wohlmann faced in getting to springs in other parts of the country.

A charabanc at Parakai Springs in 1910. Close to the vehicle is the bathhouse built by the Tourist Department in 1906. The 1900 bathhouse is at the left. *Auckland Public Library Photograph Collection.*

Without skilled medical advice and a considerable development of the baths, the Balneologist did not think "the medicinal value of the waters sufficiently high to enter into serious consideration". He added, however, that the springs were important for "pleasure purposes", the water being of a "convenient temperature".[6]

The natural spring was a timber-lined hole 0.7 m square and 2.4 m deep. A bore which had been sunk to 20 m in 1905 meant less hand pumping from the spring. The bath attendant, who lived in an old cottage near the bathhouse, received 10 shillings a week from the Domain Board and half of the bath fees.

Theoretically, the great advantage of Parakai was its proximity to Auckland. Unfortunately, at the time that Dr Wohlmann was deciding its future, the trains were unbelievably slow; it took just on 3 hours to cover the 50 km. With 6 hours' travelling time, to and from Auckland, and only 4 private baths, it is easy to believe that people sometimes returned to the city without having tried the waters. It was a factor in slowing Parakai's growth; with a fast train service Parakai might have become as significant as Waiwera, the other hot spring area close to Auckland.

A new bathhouse was built in 1906, but the £200 granted by Government didn't cover the cost of the baths themselves. For a year the new bathhouse was only a shell until, with another request and another grant, baths were placed and

This pre-1916 photograph shows, in the foreground, the swimming bath and the 2 private bath-houses. To the rear are the bowls and croquet pavilion (at left) and the 2-storeyed Parakai House, 1 of 4 well-known private hotels close to the Domain. *Alexander Turnbull Library.*

connected. Seven hundred people gathered for the opening of the new bath-house in June 1907.

After requests for money from the Helensville Domain Board in 1907 and 1908, the General Manager of the Tourist Department began to feel the Government was being led into a familiar situation where the "development goes on under Government grants and then the Board looks almost entirely to the Government for the cost of upkeep".[7]

At Helensville there were people who thought the waters were very important medicinally. There was, for example, 1 person who for 27 years had been "unable to *lay* on the right side".[8] He stayed in Mrs Goad's accommodation house, established in 1908. This was only just outside the Reserve and he spent much time in the water, and drinking it. After 3 weeks the aches and pains had left him; after 5 months he pronounced the cure a permanent one.

When a large swimming pool was built in 1909, more money had to be provided for another bore to supply it with water. The Director of Tourism was also concerned about Parakai's lack of trees: "the Baths are situated in an unkept grass paddock . . . the barren appearance and the want of shelter and amuse-ments are keeping people from the place."[9] At the same time he estimated it would cost £500 to £600 to provide quick-growing trees and tennis, croquet and bowling greens. He said he was "reluctant" to recommend the provision of that money "for the reason that this resort cannot be regarded as one of national importance".[10] So, many people did not go to Parakai at that stage because it was

Following suggestions by the Government Balneologist, the 1906 bathhouse was enlarged in 1916. By that date the Domain was developed into gardens. *Auckland Institute and Museum.*

unattractive. At the same time the Domain Board could not afford to plant trees and lay courts and greens. It was a problem familiar to many small spas; Te Puia was a good example.

There was, however, another large Parakai gathering, in 1910, to celebrate the opening of the swimming bath. The occasion was so significant that the *New Zealand Graphic* was in attendance. The reporter considered that the great drawback to Parakai was the slowness of trains on the Kaipara line — "An average speed of twelve miles an hour does not recommend itself to the modern traveller, and no sleeping cars are provided."[11]

The transformation of the Reserve began in 1910 with the planting of an avenue from the road to the baths. With another grant, work began on the greens. MP Gordon Coates championed Parakai's future in 1912, arguing that the springs were treating people unable to travel to Rotorua. When, in 1913, Cabinet examined the possibility of the Government administering Parakai's springs, the Tourist Department Manager warned that "a much more pretentious institution would be expected under Government control."[12]

Left to do the best it could with periodic Government grants, the board completed bowling and croquet greens, a tennis court, 6 ha of flower beds and shrubbery. A second accommodation house opened, with a third in 1914. Known as Parakai House and Hinemoa House, these were very much larger than the 1908 building and reflected visitors' response to better bath accommodation and more attractive surroundings.

The women's pool at Parakai (often called Helensville) in about 1950. The costumes were probably worn because of the photographer's visit — although nude and segregated bathing was the rule only in the Government spas. *Auckland Institute and Museum.*

Although the Government didn't take over Parakai, it greatly enlarged the private bathhouse, in 1916, and provided a women's swimming bath in 1924. More bores were sunk and a tea kiosk was built. Private enterprise was also busy. Springside House was opened; a pool was built at Hinemoa House. Mrs Goad's house, which became Hot Springs House, was eventually superseded by a building next to it, Craigweil House; it is now the only survivor of the Parakai accommodation houses. (The early spelling of this name appears to have been Craigweil; it is now Craigwell.)

In 1925 the Tourist Department Manager warned against further Government involvement at Parakai — "I do not want any more white elephants than we have."[13] He was undoubtedly referring to the Rotorua Bathhouse, which by 1925 was becoming a massive maintenance problem.

The late 1920s was the high point of Parakai's spa history. The Avenue, as the garden area was called, had become an attractive park. The Reserve contained 24 private baths, a men's swimming bath, one for women, Mr Brackebushe's Massage Institute (including an electrical room), a tea kiosk, bowling green, croquet lawn, tennis courts, a football ground and a games pavilion. The 4 boarding houses had baths, giving Parakai an advantage over Rotorua and Te Aroha; in at least 1 house, bathers did not have to step outside to bathe, a great

138

boon to invalids in winter. But while the accommodation and bath arrangements being under 1 roof drew people to Parakai, it also, paradoxically, took custom away from the Domain.

The onset of the Depression caused a decline in the number of visitors to Parakai. Maintenance slipped because of a lack of money and by the Second World War the spa was run down. It was almost rescued in 1948 when the Tourist Department considered taking over the Domain and Hinemoa House but the decline continued. Two of the boarding houses burned down, and the swimming baths closed in August 1958.

Redevelopment began in the 1960s. An Olympic size swimming pool opened in 1967, and the Domain is now Aquatic Park, run by a private company. Apart from a large indoor pool there is one of the largest hydroslides in the country. The site of Springside House now boasts a new thermal pool area — Palm Springs. Rickard's Tourist Complex occupies an area next to the former Hinemoa House.

The waters are still very much used but the Avenue and the old spa, with Mr Brackebushe's Massage Institute, have gone. Craigwell House is now the lone symbol of Parakai's 1920s and 1930s splendour, its leadlight Art Deco window looking out on the hydroslide of the new Parakai. As nowhere else in New Zealand, however, Craigwell House retains the cure aspect of the older style spa, providing a combination of bathing and potable mineral waters, massage, nutritional counselling and a naturopathic clinic. It is the nearest equivalent in this country to the European spas.

References

1   *Auckland Star*, February 1902.
2   Auckland Bureau to Head Office, Department of Tourist and Health Resorts, 13 March 1902. Tourist Department file 1902/41.
3   T. E. Donne, Superintendent, to Minister in charge Tourist Department, 5 September 1903. Tourist Department file 1902/41.
4   R. M. Cameron, Chairman, Helensville Domain Board, to Acting Superintendent, Department of Tourist and Health Resorts, 27 July 1905. Tourist Department file 1902/41.
5   R. M. Cameron, saddler, Helensville "and a number of others", to the Honourable the Speaker and Members of the House of Representatives, in the Parliament of New Zealand assembled, 20 September 1905. Tourist Department file 1902/41.
6   A. S. Wohlmann, Government Balneologist, to Acting Superintendent, Department of Tourist and Health Resorts, February 1906. Tourist Department file 1902/41.
7   T. E. Donne, General Manager, to the Minister for Tourist and Health Resorts, 1 September 1908. Tourist Department file 1908/117.
8   Letter to the *Wairoa Bell and Northern Advertiser*, 27 October 1908.
9   C. R. C. Robieson, Director, Division of Commerce and Tourists, Department of Agriculture, Commerce and Tourists, 23 March 1910. Tourist Department file 1908/117.
10 *Ibid*.
11 *The Weekly Graphic*, 30 March 1910.
12 General Manager to the Minister for Tourist and Health Resorts, 27 January 1913.
13 General Manager to the Minister for Tourist and Health Resorts, 13 May 1926. Tourist Department file 122/1.

21 Kamo Springs

Kamo is New Zealand's almost forgotten spa. The area has always had difficulties competing with other springs because of a lack of really hot water. The mineral water at Kamo Springs has a temperature of only 25°C, which is not considered hot enough by most hot pool bathers. It was, however, 1 of the most popular drinking waters. The place was well advertised, it had an attractive setting and it was close to a large town.

Kamo was first publicised by well-known photographer Josiah Martin. In the 1880s and 1890s, he made journeys from his studio and shop in Auckland's Queen Street to record landscapes in geothermal areas and he is best known for his work associated with the Volcanic Plateau. As early as 1879 he wrote an extensive article on the Rotomahana Terraces and another piece, which includes the most detailed description of the terraces, was the result of an 1883 lecture he delivered to the Geological Society of London.

Martin's 1883 guide to Whangarei and Kamo drew attention to cold chalybeate springs (chalybeate waters contain iron) 9 km north-west of Whangarei. "The township of Kamo is a celebrated health resort . . . near the road side are the celebrated Soda Water Springs where a cooling draught of chalybeate water can be obtained." Martin added: "Although we usually recommend Temperance drinks, the popular verdict is that these waters are more palatable when qualified with something stronger."[1]

Henry Winkelmann, another important Auckland photographer, recorded the Kamo area in 1902. Apart from his photographs of the Hauraki Gulf, Winkelmann was probably the most important early mountaineering photographer in the North Island. Almost every photographer who visited the north took pictures of the curiously shaped limestone rocks at Kamo.

Mr J. J. Taylor, the owner of a property on Springs Flat near Kamo, is credited with discovering the main springs in 1889, supposedly while burying a horse. This image tends to conjure up, incorrectly, the idea of surface trickles, whereas the two springs on this property are considerably the largest in the area and it is extremely unlikely that the Ngapuhi people were unaware of the water before Mr Taylor's horse died. There is also an analysis of water from this area, by J. Pond, dating from 1878,[2] though his sample was possibly taken from one of the less significant springs. Mr Taylor's claim was published in the *Cyclopedia of New Zealand*, an often inaccurate source.

Kamo Springs advertised in Thomas Cook's *New Zealand as a Tourist and Health Resort*, 1902. It
is now almost forgotten that the area was once a spa. *Canterbury Public Library.*

The supposed discoverer made improvements around the springs and opened them to the public in 1894. The facilities included a "well-lighted" swimming basin and the Electric Bath.[3] This was so named not because an electric current was conducted through the water, as was the case with some of the Rotorua baths, but because of the tingling sensation brought about by gas bubbles, which rose through the pool so that it appeared to be violently boiling. Even though the temperature was only 23.9°C bathers maintained that the pool eased rheumatic aches. (In Rotorua people considered 37.8°C the minimum temperature for rheumatic problems and sought temperatures as high as 43.3°C.)

According to the *Cyclopedia*, large numbers of people were visiting the springs daily by 1902, people who spoke "in the highest praise" of the medicinal value of the waters. As with every springs area, there were records of seemingly miraculous recoveries at Kamo; people who were carried to the pools were "completely cured in a fortnight."[4] The water was drunk for dyspepsia because it contained a considerable amount of calcium carbonate and sodium carbonate. Kamo water was also believed to be a very efficient solvent of "red gravel" (in the kidneys).

When Mr Taylor bought the property with the main springs in 1870, he was 1 of only 4 private individuals who purchased the title to hot springs before the Lands and Survey Department could declare the area a scenic reserve. The department became concerned with hot springs from 1880 onwards while Rolleston was Minister. Apart from Kamo, it was only at Waiwera, Wairakei and Taupo that Lands and Survey were too late to secure hot springs for the Government.

At Kamo a 4 ha block was reserved by the department in 1886. Small springs on this block fed a bath, but it was no competition for the major springs at Taylor's establishment. When the Tourist Department took over Government interests in hot springs, Dr Wohlmann, keen to have access to any waters which might be useful medicinally, wished that Kamo was closer to Rotorua. He considered that in England Kamo water would be "of immense value".[5] On the Volcanic Plateau, where the Government was developing the Rotorua spa, there was a lack of a good drinking water.

Another advantage of the Kamo Springs, according to Wohlmann, was the amount of gas rising through the water. Gas baths were becoming very popular in Continental spas at this time. Kamo's Electric Bath, later called the Champagne Bath, contained enough gas, the Balneologist thought, to make hundreds of gas baths. "The gas is the great therapeutic agent at Kamo"[6] he wrote, suggesting that the gas be caught and recharged into the waters of all the baths there.

Most reports relating to Wohlmann's work were written in the light of partisan interests, so an *Auckland Star* article on the doctor's 1903 visit to Kamo is refreshing in its lack of references to local resources being ignored by the Government:

He takes a very thorough interest in his work and nothing seems to be too trivial or too laborious for him . . . The cheerful manner in which he visited different persons' properties to pass opinion in regard to their springs quite charmed everybody who came in contact with the eminent balneologist and it does not require any great foresight to see that the doctor will become very popular wherever he goes. He is an Englishman of the best school.[7]

Kamo Sanatorium and bathhouses, 1905. It was a sanatorium in name only as there was no medical staff. *Photograph by Muir and Moodie, National Museum.*

Cook's guide of 1905 contained an extensive description of the small Kamo spa. Besides 1 natural bath, there were 2 swimming baths and 4 private baths, the latter artificially heated. Spring water was heated in tanks by steam forced through copper coils, a process which went against the whole balneological principle of using water that was as natural as possible. (This belief in natural spring water was particularly strong in Rotorua where people considered that water in a natural spring was more valuable than the same water piped to a nearby bath.)

At Kamo Springs the natural bath was "the stronger — a bathhouse has been built over a very powerful mineral spring which has been dug out and walled with wood".[8] The swimming bath had water piped into it from the drinking spring.

A hotel was opened next to the springs in 1905 to complement the accommodation house known as the Sanatorium. The Cook's article stated that the new building met "the wants of those who prefer a hotel to the quieter method of living catered for at the Sanatorium".[9] The former Medical Officer at Rotorua, Dr Hope Lewis, added his opinion to the article. He asserted that Kamo water rendered the bile more fluid and "imparted more elasticity" to the liver.[10] It was also efficacious in the case of a Mr Kennedy who had damaged his kidneys through "excessive indulgence in amateur athletics".[11]

After the Whangarei Chamber of Commerce pressed the Government to purchase Kamo Springs the Balneologist made a second visit in 1907. This time the doctor described the 25°C waters as tepid and "foaming with a fierce effervescence of gas".[12] While charged with carbonic acid the water was crystal clear but when it was artificially heated the gas was lost and iron oxide gave the water a

A 1907 photograph of Kamo showing, from left, the women's bathhouse, the pump for drawing mineral water, the men's bath and the Champagne Bath. The ramp was related to the sale of Kamo water. *Alexander Turnbull Library.*

red discolouration. Because the carbonic acid bubbles in the natural pools stimulated the skin and "materially" assisted the circulation of the blood, "thereby relieving the heart",[13] Wohlmann considered that Kamo could become the Nauheim of New Zealand. (The famous German spa specialises in treating heart conditions.) Another advantage of the carbonic acid gas was that, owing to the stimulation of the skin, invalids were able to take baths at a lower temperature than if the gas were absent.

The Champagne Bath, built over the main spring, was the only bath of special therapeutic value, according to the doctor. It had to be used with care, however. The amount of carbon dioxide, discharged within the confined space, occasionally suffocated bathers by displacing oxygen. All the other baths were supplied from the drinking spring.

Kamo's drinking water was sent to Auckland where it was bottled, but Dr Wohlmann believed it was diluted with distilled water and that some of the iron was removed — "iron blackens whiskey,"[14] he explained. The Sanatorium was one in name only, he claimed; there was no provision for medical attendance or nursing.

Overall, however, the Balneologist advised the Government to buy Kamo Springs, not only because it was the best representative of a particular type of water but also for the sake of public safety — there had been several deaths in the Champagne Bath.

Two matters in Wohlmann's report probably decided the Government against Kamo. The Balneologist had suggested the need for nursing and recommended that the Sanatorium might succeed with another 12 beds. In 1907, however, the Government was in the process of erecting the Rotorua Bathhouse, at the huge

The Kamo Springs Hotel provided more comfort than the Sanatorium until it was destroyed by fire in 1915. *Photograph by Frank Radcliffe, Alexander Turnbull Library.*

cost of £40,000; there was no money to spare. The second matter concerned the purchase of land. Dr Wohlmann suggested it might be necessary to buy more land to guarantee the flow of spring water. (The Sanatorium was surrounded by a considerable number of small springs.) The landowner immediately asked £1,000 per 0.4 ha for the 1.2 ha involved. This was on top of the £19,000 being asked for the Sanatorium, baths and 18 ha. If the Government had been asked to pay £10,000 instead of £22,000, they might have bought Kamo and made it into another Morere, but the price was too high.

The extent and the quality of the Rotorua Bathhouse fittings gave landowners of hot springs areas throughout the country the impression that the Government could pay top market prices for property. At the same time as Kamo was being offered for £22,000, Wairakei was being offered for £30,000. The Government simply couldn't afford these amounts.

Another factor which weighed against Kamo's future was that the Government was already spending money on baths at Parakai near Helensville, only 130 km away. The deaths that had occurred in the Champagne Bath were the final deciding factor. In 1902, a man died in the bathhouse exactly 12 months to the day after the manager's wife had died there from "carbonic acid gas poisoning".[15] The bathhouses and Sanatorium all needed expensive reconstruction.

When the Government decided, at the end of 1907, not to purchase, Kamo, without a Robert Graham or a company to promote and develop it, had to turn to a local deputation. A group of Whangarei people went to the Government in 1910, only to be told by the Minister for Tourist and Health Resorts that the Government was already "being censured for its expenditure".[16] (In fact, the Government's refusal to buy Kamo Springs for £19,000 was reasonable in the light of later valuations. When the hotel and Sanatorium were put up for auction in 1915, the purchaser announced that he would accept £2,000 for the Sanatorium, the baths and 5 ha.)

From 1905 additional accommodation at the springs had been provided in the 20-roomed Kamo Springs Hotel, but this short-lived building burned down in September 1915. The Sanatorium took on a special role in 1918 and 1919 when it was adapted for convalescent returned troops. It was useful for some cases not suited to Rotorua's sulphur fumes. Fifty soldiers were housed at a time.

As a result, the Whangarei Hospital Board purchased the property in 1920, for £4,500. Unfortunately 1 of the returned soliders died that year from the carbon dioxide displacement of oxygen in one of the bathhouses. By 1929 the hospital board wanted to get rid of the property. The Government was approached by the Manager of the Tourist Department and warned that if the Government developed Kamo Springs and Ngawha Springs as well as the other North Auckland spa area, Parakai, the 3 areas would compete for a limited clientele. Such a move would also create the expense of several staffs.

The spa was advertised for tender in April 1929, but without success. It was leased out in 1932 and sold in 1936 for £1,200. Admittedly the Kamo Springs property offered for £19,000 in 1907 included a small hotel and more farmland, but the reduction in price reflected the change of attitude towards spas that had taken place in the intervening years. This was partly the result of an economic depression.

The Sanatorium became a tearooms as the centre for an attractive recreational area, including tennis courts and a large open-air swimming pool. In the 1940s, however, a strange remnant of the old atmosphere still lingered: an old man dispensed spring water to customers. He would run down steps to the drinking spring, dip cups into the water and then hold his breath as he raced back up the steps. This practice ended when a child was overcome by the carbon dioxide at the bottom of the steps and the spring was boarded over. Much earlier, the women's bathhouse was shut up, after a tragedy involving a mother and daughter.

The place was very dangerous for bathing, but largely because none of the owners was able to provide the money to build atmosphere-controlled bathhouses.

A religious group bought the area in 1980. A church and school cover the site of the open-air pool; the Sanatorium building is now a pastor's house. Only the Champagne Pool remains in use. In 1911 Dr Wohlmann wrote "the one spring above all others outside the Thermal District which we should have a lien over, under any circumstances, is Kamo."[17] He would find Kamo unrecognisable today.

References

1   Martin, J. *Guide to Whangarei & Kamo*, 1888.
2   Pond, J. A. 'Notes on a salt spring near Hokianga' in *Transactions of the New Zealand Institute*, Vol. XI, 1878, p. 513.

3   *The Cyclopedia of New Zealand*, 1902.
4   *Ibid.*
5   *Auckland Star*, 5 August 1903.
6   *Ibid.*
7   *Ibid.*
8   Cook, J. *New Zealand as a Tourist and Health Resort*, 5th ed., 1905.
9   *Ibid.*
10 *Ibid.*
11 *The Northern Advocate*, 6 October 1903.
12 Dr Wohlmann. Report on Kamo Springs 1907. Tourist Department files.
13 *Ibid.*
14 *Ibid.*
15 *New Zealand Herald*, 19 June 1902.
16 *Northern Mail*, 6 May 1910.
17 Dr Wohlmann, 6 June 1911. Tourist Department files.

22 Ngawha

Nineteenth-century visitors who had taken the cure at European or British spas must have found some of New Zealand's watering places dismal by comparison. Quite apart from the sometimes primitive, or even non-existent, facilities, the surrounding scenery of manuka, brown and yellow sulphur mounds or grey silica flats must have seemed like a landscape from another world. Even within New Zealand, such areas contrasted markedly with the green native forest that covered much of the country.

Ngawha, 7 km from Kaikohe, may well have appeared like an ulcer in the countryside and it did not improve until the 1930s. The place has never been a fashionable spa, nor a part of the country's tourist network. Had it been closer to the Bay of Islands, a Sheraton, a Hyatt Kingsgate, or a Tourist Hotel Corporation building might perhaps have been built at Ngawha in the last 10 years. Although, because of its isolation from tourist routes, it has remained an area of mainly local significance, there has always been a number of enthusiasts who believe Ngawha's muds and waters are more effective than any others in New Zealand in treating rheumatic ailments and skin complaints.

The Ngawha springs are in an old lake basin, the several groups of geothermal activity marking the sites of former streams which drained that lake. There are mudpools, gas vents and hot water pools, and the waters are mainly acidic, many containing a small proportion of sulphuric acid. What is unusual about this area is a deposit of cinnabar or mercuric sulphide. For many years claims were made about the curative powers of the mercuric Ngawha mud, principally for the treatment of syphilis. Mercury is no longer used for that purpose, but Ngawha mud also seems to have been effective in clearing up skin complaints.

Written accounts of bathing in Ngawha's hot waters and muds go back to the missionary, William Wade, who in his *A Journey in the Northern Island of New Zealand*, 1842, noted: "The springs at this place are much resorted to by diseased natives from the Bay of Islands, who bring baskets of provisions with them, and remain on the spot to use the sulphur warm-bath till a cure is effected."[1] Apart from an analysis of Ngawha water in 1869, literature relating to the area is comparatively recent. The Government Balneologist's *The Hot Springs of New Zealand*, published in 1921, referred to "a remarkable group of hot springs at Ohaewai [Ohaeawai is 5 km from Ngawha] . . . in the midst of old workings of a mercury mine, itself desolate in a setting of old gum fields." He wrote of the hot mud, containing globules of cinnabar, being used as a parasiticide by Maori people of

148

Ngawha Curative Springs in about 1935. At the rear are remnants of mercury extraction operations. *Photograph by J. Batchelor, Rotorua Museum.*

the area. "At present", he explained, "these baths are unused."[2] What he meant was that at the time he visited them, sometime between 1902 and 1918, there were no bathhouses there, no doctor, no bathing regulations and no European bathers. The combination of mud, cinnabar and sulphurous water would, he believed, have made the authorities at Aachen envious. (Aachen, at one time known as Aix-la-Chapelle, is one of the most important sulphurous water spas in Europe.)

As Ngawha is the largest and most active group of springs outside the Volcanic Plateau, North Auckland residents undoubtedly wondered why the Government appeared to take no interest in this resource until the 1940s. At the most important period of spa development in the country, 1901-08, the Tourist Department's preoccupation with Rotorua was partly responsible for the lack of interest in the far north. It was also partly a matter of population. There is a much greater range of waters at Ngawha than at Parakai near Helensville or at Kamo Springs near Whangarei, but these spas had the advantage of proximity to large population centres and so were developed mainly for this reason. (Parakai is 50 km from Auckland, Kamo is 9 km from Whangarei, Waiwera is 40 km north of Auckland.)

Ngawha was also left undeveloped until the 1950s because of its lack of attractive scenery. It is perhaps only poets, artists and misanthropes who tend to enjoy bleak views, but there have never been enough of them to ensure the financial success of an austere and lonely spa. Only the upper level of pools at Tikitere and the thermal area at Rotokawa near Taupo can match Ngawha for sombreness of view.

Blair, the third Government Balneologist, had forebodings about Ngawha's landscape in 1944. At that stage the Government had become interested in Ngawha after learning that a company was being formed to develop the springs.

In considering the area's possibilities, Blair explained that the road to the spa "runs through desolate scenery". In fact, one of his chief objections to the development of Ngawha was "the gloomy and desolate appearance of the surroundings".[3]

Blair was also concerned about patients using the same water over and over again — the baths at that stage were holes dug in the ground with little overflow. At the same time, he believed that no other waters in North Auckland were suitable for treating rheumatism. Other features in Ngawha's favour were the range in its waters from moderate acidity to moderate alkalinity, and the variety of salts, from carbonates to chlorides and sulphates. Blair warned, however, against placing too much emphasis upon the mineral content of spa waters. The effect of mineral baths depends largely, he pointed out,

> on the action of heat plus moisture applied locally and generally for a prolonged period: the salts in solution merely adding to the effect . . . it appears to be of little importance whether these dissolved salts are chlorides, carbonates or sulphates . . . The major exception to this is the presence of free sulphuric acid, which has a definite effect upon the skin, and the surface circulation.[4]

Unfortunately for Ngawha, at the time of Blair's inspection, the 1 pool in the area with a considerable amount of free sulphuric acid was in an upper valley, inaccessible to invalids. What prevented any probability of Government development of Ngawha was the disclosure that, with little or no overflow of water in the pools, there could be no sophisticated treatment building; such an establishment would require a considerable volume of hot mineral water. Blair suggested that the area could be a useful adjunct to the treatment of rheumatism in hospitals. This suggestion, in turn, depended upon easy access to Ngawha; until the 1950s the last few kilometres to the springs amounted to nothing more than a rough track.

Faced with the reconstruction of the Rotorua Bathhouse and Sanatorium, at a cost of at least £150,000, the Government was not, in 1944, very interested in Ngawha. The Health Department was not much more enthusiastic. After a visit to Ngawha in November 1948, Dr Lennane, Director of Physical Medicine, reported: "In view of the slow flow of water through the baths and the fact that they have a reputation for healing or curing skin diseases, it would seem undesirable for a large number of patients to pass through the bath in any one day."[5]

He described the area behind the Spa Hotel as "desolate" with "various bubbling mud pools of a most revolting aspect".[6] People immersed themselves in these, but there was no means of removing the mud after immersion except by getting into a pool where the mud was a little less thick. (These bathing conditions were similar to those at Rotorua's Sulphur Point area 70 years before Lennane's visit to Ngawha — but with an important difference: at Rotorua the lake, where the mud could easily be washed off, was only a few metres away.) Among the Ngawha mudpools was the Tiger Bath, renowned for the relief it gave to rheumatic conditions. Access was the problem: "Patients who do not have full use of their limbs might easily meet with a serious accident on their way,"[7] Dr Lennane warned.

The Tiger Bath at Ngawha. The cinnabar in this mud was effective in the treatment of skin complaints. *Alexander Turnbull Library.*

The main spa area consisted of 8 excavated baths, with boarded sides and sand bottoms, known as the Velvet, the Twin, the Jubilee, the Lobster, the Waipiro, the Barnard, the Cinnabar and the Annie. There was considerable communication of waters beneath several of these pools. After examining the other groups of baths in the valley, Dr Lennane summed up his attitude to Ngawha. There were no advantages over Rotorua for the treatment of rheumatic diseases, and there were several disadvantages, including poor access, distance from a large centre of population, and an insufficient fresh water supply.

When examined by geologists, and the Balneologist in 1944, the other group of pools included the Rata (Doctor), the Horomona, the Waikato, the Bulldog and the Peipei. There was disagreement over who owned some of these pools. They are divided between what was known, in nearby Kaikohe, as "the Maori side" (of a corrugated iron fence) or "the Maori acre" and the Domain pools, an area of 1.6 ha. The "acre" is still controlled by the Ngawha Springs Trust, a tribal committee of the Ngaiatawhake and Te Uriohua people, who also claimed ownership of the 1.6 ha administered since 1935 by the Ngawha Springs Domain Board. A petition was taken to the Government in 1945 to have the Domain area vested in the Ngawha Springs Trust. It was, however, unsuccessful. Both springs areas have been considerably upgraded over the last 30 years.

The spa area of 283 ha, owned at various times by Cunningham (when it was known as Cunningham's Curative Hot Springs), Jolson and Ginn, for many years had the only hotel near the springs. There was a second hotel near the Domain between 1956 and 1983.

This thermal area at Ngawha, photographed in c. 1935, is the bed of an ancient lake.
Photograph by J. Batchelor, Rotorua Museum.

In all hot springs bathing areas in New Zealand there are 2 opinions as to the efficacy of the waters: the official and the local. In Ngawha's case this is particularly so.

Frank Robson's *Amazing Story of Ngawha's Hot Mercurial Health Springs* tells the story of Bill Bradford. Mr Bradford was brought to Ngawha on a stretcher, crippled with arthritis, "a sort of living skeleton".[8] As another bather recalled, "all he could move seemed to be his eyelids. He had to be carried to the pools on a stretcher, and lowered into the water."[9] He was actually put into the water on his stretcher. Eventually he was placed in the Favourite, the hottest pool, for 10 minutes at a time. He would emerge, looking half-boiled, but able to move his limbs a little. Soon he could move sideways, like a crab, from pool to pool. Two years later he seemed completely cured. Bradford himself, however, felt that diet had been partly responsible for his recovery.

Other local opinions included statements from doctors in the area. "For many years I was a dermatologist . . . when I have got to the end of my tether with local treatment, I send them to Ngawha; it would be quite useless to send them to Rotorua. The unique value of the mercury sulphide hot waters of the place, elsewhere in the world, would be recognised and developed."[10] (Actually, analyses in 1944 failed to find any mercury in Ngawha waters, although it is present in the mud.) Dr Pettit had this to say: "In 1942 I was senior Medical Officer in that area and used the springs for the troops. The response to treatment of skin eruptions was remarkable and far better than any other known treatment."[11] The official attitude was, however, influenced by the opinion of the Director of Physical Medicine, who wrote in October 1955:

> The clamour for the development of these springs is wholly of local origin. Nobody living any distance away is likely to support them. I would estimate that it would cost at least £100,000 to build a suitable hotel, ensure an adequate water supply, and provide drainage. I really think the project is impracticable and likely to become a heavy burden on the Government eventually.[12]

Government interest in the area is now limited to the Ministry of Energy's trial drilling for the possibility of a geothermal power station similar to Wairakei and Ohaaki. This will probably affect the natural surface activity and the baths. The "acre" has become Waiariki Pools, and the Domain is now administered by the Bay of Islands County Council. The Spa Hotel still welcomes its adherents from several countries.

Perhaps, if the geothermal energy scheme eventuates, future visitors to the site will one day be shown remnants of Ngawha's spa history, just as today's visitors examine traces of 1890s and 1920s mercury mining, and a few wisps of steam will recall a history of bathing in this strange landscape.

References

1   Wade, William. *A Journey in the Northern Island of New Zealand*, Hobart, Rolwegan, 1842.
2   Herbert, A. S. *The Hot Springs of New Zealand*, London, Lewis, 1921.
3   Report by Dr Blair, Balneologist, Rotorua, for Department of Industries and Commerce, Tourist and Publicity, March 1944. Tourist Department file 20/55.
4   *Ibid*.
5   G. A. Q. Lennane, Director of Physical Medicine, to Director General of Health, December 1948. Department of Health file 177/42.
6   *Ibid*.
7   *Ibid*.
8   Robson, Frank N. "The amazing story of Ngawha's hot mercurial health springs" in *Bay of Islands Annual 1956*.
9   *Ibid*.
10 Dr H. W. Wilson, Kaikohe, to Minister of Health, 13 August 1953. Tourist Department file 20/55.
11 Dr H. Pettit, Auckland in *Bay of Islands Annual 1956*.
12 G. A. Q. Lennane, Director, Division of Physical Medicine, to Minister of Health, 4 October 1955. Health Department file 5/1/1.

23 More Springs on the Plateau

There are more geothermal springs suitable for bathing on the Volcanic Plateau than in all the rest of New Zealand. They are scattered in small groups from Taheke, north of Rotoiti, to Tarawera on the Napier-Taupo Road, and from Rotoehu to Atiamuri. Several other groups of springs lie just off the edge of the Plateau, such as Okoroire to the north and Onepu, at Kawerau, to the east. Most of the springs on the Plateau are surrounded by silica deposits; most of those elsewhere are not, although there are exceptions — the Waikite Springs on the Plateau are surrounded by clay only, while the Onepu Springs on the edge of the Tarawera River Valley have a considerable silica deposit.

Several of the Plateau springs, apart from those at Sulphur Point, Wairakei, Taupo or Tokaanu, were very important bathing places for tourists from 1860 until around the Second World War. The 2 most important centres were Ohinemutu and Whakarewarewa which, although they were not developed as spas in the European sense, both had a wide reputation for their waters.

For several centuries, before Europeans brought the spa concept to this country, Ohinemutu probably had the greatest single reputation of all New Zealand's hot water bathing places, with some competition from Tokaanu, Waiwera and Ngawha. A way of life developed around the warm bathing pools (wai-ariki) of this large village spreading from the Papaiouru Marae to Muruika Point (the present site of St Faith's Church) and up to Pukeroa (the site of Rotorua's Public Hospital).

Sir William Fox described the edge of the lake at Ohinemutu in 1874:

Rotorua affords facilities for bathing 'in the open' on the largest scale of any single place in the hot spring districts. The whole bay in front of Ohinemutu . . . some hundred yards across, has a temperature of from 50° to 100° [Fahrenheit] according to the set of the wind and the proximity to the hot springs by which it is fed . . . This bay is the daily resort, morning and evening, of the whole population of the neighbouring village, and it is capable of accommodating regiments of soldiers at one time. It affords the finest conceivable opportunity of establishing a great sanatorium for Indian regiments."[1]

No one else took New Zealand's position as a watering hole for the Empire quite so seriously as Fox. James Cowan, in *The Maoris of New Zealand*, published in 1910, was more concerned with the sociological rather than the balneological aspects of Ohinemutu: "Ruapeka, the little sandy bay at Ohinemutu . . . was the great bathing place . . . Here in the pleasant warm waters, heated by many hot springs, practically the whole population would gather in the evenings for social gossip and song. It was the most unconventional of 'musical evenings'."[2]

A romantic view of Ruapeka Bay, Ohinemutu, in the 1870s, with Waikite Geyser looking like a fireworks display. Illustration from H. Meade, *A Ride Through the Disturbed Districts of New Zealand*, Rotorua Museum.

Cowan's account was particularly interesting in its claim that, at Ruapeka, there was a dispensation from the moral codes of Maori society: "There is a local proverbial saying that indicates the free-and-easy conditions which obtained amongst this water-loving tribe, where mixed bathing was the fashion — 'Kaore he ture ki Ruapeka' — 'There is no law in Ruapeka'."[3] Cowan explained that any man who wished to keep his wife to himself should keep her away from Ruapeka, adding: "But as the husband often preferred to indemnify himself by making love under cover of darkness and the steam to someone else's wife, matters were adjusted all round and everyone was very merry in Ruapeka Bay."[4]

Most European visitors accepted the mixed nude bathing at Ohinemutu and elsewhere without too many qualms. A few visitors, however, seemed to feel it was their duty to affect shock and disapproval. In 1888 A. D. Willis came across some young Maori women in a pool:

> Apparently (for, of course, I averted my eyes at once) they wore nothing but smiles, and as at the best this kind of garment must be considered flimsy, we were much shocked and our natural sense of modesty suggested we should fly from the place at once. The young ladies, finding themselves discovered in this unexpected fashion, burst into a hearty laugh, and shouted an invitation to join them. The whole thing was so indecorous that it is quite needless to say we did not avail ourselves of the kindly offer, but fled the spot.[5]

In 1883 Robert Graham built a large bathhouse at Ohinemutu for his Lake House Hotel and smaller bathhouses were provided by the other hotels. Only the local people recall the names of former hot pools. The spring used by the Lake House was known as Waihunuhunukuri — "water for scalding a dog". Such names were difficult for travellers and bland English titles were often substituted. The Lake View Hotel, for example, called its bathhouse the Premier.

The Newest GUIDE TO THE HOT LAKES, BY A MAN CONSTANTLY IN HOT WATER.

This 1882 brochure designed to advertise the Palace Hotel at Ohinemutu was a reply to Thorpe Talbot's *A Month in Hot Water*, which extolled the virtues of Robert Graham's Lake House Hotel, also at Ohinemutu. The guide was typical of literature relating to the Hot Lakes district, as the area around Rotorua was known in the 1880s. *Auckland Institute and Museum Library*.

156

Ohinemutu, c. 1900, showing 1 of the bathing pools, fed from a hotter ngawha to the rear. The small building is a private bathhouse for either Morrison's Rotorua Hotel or Seddon's Lake View. *Photograph by Josiah Martin, Auckland Institute and Museum.*

Fortunately, there were plenty of pools available for bathing. Otherwise the situation mentioned by Clement Bunbury in 1879 — "I tried a natural bath which has been inclosed by the hotel-keeper to keep out the natives"[6] — could have resulted in the same sort of tensions that developed at Tokaanu. The Waikite pool area in Ruapeka Bay dried up and the bathing pools that remain at Ohinemutu are now enclosed as family bathhouses.

The area that most appealed to the Victorian imagination and sense of wonder was Rotomahana, with its extraordinary Pink and White Terraces. Described as the eighth wonder of the world, they were responsible for the beginnings of tourism in New Zealand, but even before large numbers of visitors arrived to view these phenomena, their reputation as bathing places was established after an 1847 report by Dr Johnson: "It was indeed such a luxurious amusement that we could not refrain from plunging in again and again, after we had intended to come out."[7]

The great advantage of bathing at the Terraces was the choice of temperature, according to the distance of a terrace from the cauldron. As J. Ernest Tinne recalled in 1872 in *The Wonders of the Antipodes*: "Did you require additional warmth you had but to take a step towards the great blue depths of the geyser, whence the water flowed down into successive basins . . ."[8]

In the same year Anthony Trollope, in *Australia and New Zealand*, 1873, exhibited an uncharacteristic sensuousness after bathing in the Pink Terrace pools: "The lips and sides of the baths are tinged with that delicate pink hue

Otukapuarangi or the Pink Terrace, photographed about 1880. This terrace was preferred for bathing because of the greater number of hot pools deep enough for swimming. The smoothness of its silica formations reminded some bathers of alabaster.

which one is apt to connect with voluptuous enjoyment. The baths are . . . like vast open shells, the walls of which are concave, and the lips ornamented in a thousand forms . . . I have never heard of other bathing like this in the world."[9]

Trollope was, however, worried about the proprieties of such bathing:

> I was somewhat troubled by the future bathing arrangements. To enclose the various basins would spoil them altogether to the eye. To dabble about in vestments arranged after some French fashion would spoil the bathing to the touch. And yet it must be open to men and women alike. The place lies so broad to the world's eye, that I fear no arrangement as to hours, no morning for the gents, and evening for the ladies would suffice . . . The ladies indeed, might have the Pink, and the men the White Terrace; but the intervening lake would discourage social intercourse . . .[10]

So unusual were the Terraces that Fox, the most important nineteenth-century advocate of spas in New Zealand, had reservations about their development: "the idea that these majestic scenes may one day be desecrated by all the constituents of a common watering-place has something in it bordering on profanity."[11] Thorpe Talbot, in her *Geysers and Gazers* of 1882, recorded a more vulgar description of the delights of bathing in the Terraces. She claimed to have heard a woman describe the "toot onsomble" as "altogether too bewilderingly, exquisitely, consummately oh fay for anything!"[12]

James Anthony Froude, close to 70 when he visited Rotomahana, wrote after bathing in the Pink Terrace: "I, for one, when I was dressed again, could have

The White Terrace, c. 1880. "The Hole in the Wall" basin in this photograph was the usual bathing pool of Te Tarata or the White Terrace. *Alexander Turnbull Library*.

fancied myself back in the old days when I did not know that I had a body, and could run up hill as lightly as down."[13] He was responsible for the most beautiful description of the Terraces in his 1885 *Oceana*, although it is very similar to a passage in Alfred Domett's epic poem, *Ranolf and Amohia*, written in 1872. Froude describes the pool, Otukapuarangi, at the top of the Pink Terrace:

> The hue of the water was something which I had never seen, and I shall never see again on this side of eternity. Not the violet, not the hare-bell, nearest in its tint to heaven of all nature's flowers; not turquoise, not sapphire, not the unfathomable aether itself could convey to one who had not looked on it a sense of that supernatural loveliness.[14]

Here is Domett's earlier response to the same scene:

Each terrace a wide basin brimmed
With water, brilliant, yet in hue
The tenderest delicate harebell-blue
Deepening to violet . . .[15]

The White Terrace contained only 1 basin of hot water deep enough for swimming; the Pink Terrace had 5. Apart from this, the Pink Terrace was preferred for its smoother surface.

The Romans created a spa, Hierapolis, at Pamukkale in Turkey, the only other place in the world that resembles the former Terraces. Had Tarawera not erupted in 1886 and the Terraces been destroyed, bathing sheds and hotels would have extended the Rotorua spa out to Rotomahana and, perhaps, in the 1980s, steel water chutes would have carried shrieking children to various levels of the pools.

159

This turn of the century photograph of Tikitere shows the Te Mimi-o-te-Kakahi waterfall much used as a spout bath. This area almost became New Zealand's first spa in 1849. *Rotorua Museum.*

The attempt to create a spa at Tikitere failed because of intertribal land claims. Preliminary investigation took place in January 1847 when Dr Johnson, the Colonial Surgeon, walked over the thermal area and recorded the following in his journal: "The valley I have described would appear well situated for the site of the hospital which His Excellency the Governor proposes to erect in this part of the country . . ."[16] Grey had obviously been considering such a hospital for treating rheumatic patients some time before his visit to Rotorua and Tikitere in July 1848. Thomas Chapman, the missionary at nearby Te Ngae, noted: "The mind of the Governor was to benefit the natives and probably to see how far an infant Cheltenham might be introduced."[17]

Almost 40 years later there was a small private spa at Tikitere under the management of a Mr McRory. It consisted simply of a raupo whare to accommodate patients, who usually bathed in Te Mimi-o-te-Kakahi, the hot waterfall between the 2 levels of Tikitere. There was also a whare-covered bath near the accommodation, fed by the Huritini Pool. Dr Hope Lewis, the Medical Officer at Rotorua, advised: "It is well not to visit Tikitere alone, as the isolation is extreme and the general aspect of the place is calculated to produce a fit of melancholy."[18] Depression wasn't the only danger at Tikitere. In November 1881, when the sulphur beds caught fire, the whare and bathhouses were burned down and some invalids were nearly suffocated, losing their clothes and all their possessions. Some people, however, defied both depression and sulphur. The 1898 *New Zealand Tours and Excursions* claimed that "invalids, even ladies, live here for

Whakarewarewa's original bathhouse at Turikore pool. Built in 1894 by the manager of the Geyser Hotel, it was replaced by a larger structure. *Photograph by R. Thompson, Rotorua Art Gallery.*

weeks in order to benefit by the valuable mud and other baths which have effected so many cures".[19] In the late nineteenth century Tikitere had an advantage over many of the thermal areas on the Plateau — it was close to a farm and people staying for the treatment could obtain fresh meat and milk.

Whakarewarewa, too, had whares which were let to visiting invalids taking a course of baths. It is first mentioned in *Maoriland*, an 1884 guide book. Dr Hope Lewis commented in 1885: "the Maoris at this place take great interest in the patients who rent their whares and live amongst them for the benefit of the baths. They are most facile in the handling of cripples, and can be engaged in such cases to be always in attendance during the bath."[20] The baths most commonly used were Turikore, or the Spout Bath, and Korotiotio, the Oil Bath. In 1894 the manager of the Geyser Hotel built simple bathhouses at both sites, the one at Turikore being replaced by a handsome Government structure in 1909. The water supply failed at the end of 1942 and the bathhouse was dismantled 4 years later. The Oil Bath building was removed when a particular hotel manager failed to pay the rent on it. The open baths are still there. The aluminium sulphate in the Alum Bath at Te Kiri Parewhangi, a small pool south of the village, was helpful in treating haemorrhoids. Visiting writers often confused this pool with the Alum Fall Bath north of the village, in the area that was to become the Rotorua airfield.

The recent indications of a lowering water table at Whakarewarewa could have disastrous effects on the village in 2 ways. First, it could alter the scenic geothermal activity and hence the economy of the whole area; second, it could mean

161

The second Spout Bathhouse at Whakarewarewa was opened in February 1909. It was built by the Government but leased to the owners of the Geyser Hotel. The water supply failed at the end of 1942 and the building was demolished in 1946. *Photograph by Lawrence Birks, Resident Engineer, Rotorua, 1906–10, Rotorua Museum.*

the communal baths could not be used. This would have serious consequences for a village where many of the houses have no bathrooms. For a short time, not long ago, the communal pools at the site of the old Oil Bath could not be used because the water level was too low. If the situation were permanent many Whakarewarewa people would have to move. Then we would have only photographs, from 1885 (when Alfred Burton was in the area) until around 1930 (when photographs of bathing in the village were no longer taken as the villagers required more privacy) to remind us of the famous bathing pools of Whakarewarewa.

Separated from Whakarewarewa by a narrow rib of firm ground is a group of mudpools and lakelets. Some of the pools now make interesting traps for Arikikapakapa golfers, but before its golf course days this thermal area had a brief history of mudpool cures. An 1878 guide book mentioned that Arikikapakapa "has one or two baths of intensely acidulous water, occasionally used by infants". (The guide did not explain what the infants used it for.) The book also mentioned that: "the Honourable Mr Bertie, who suffered from spinal disease, was cured in one of the mud-holes."[21] It was claimed in 1902 that water from Jack's Bath at Arikikapakapa was good for "sandy blight and other diseases of the eye common to Australia".[22] The bath was used until the First World War but no trace of it remains today and the writer has been unable to find anyone who knows its site.

It is now almost forgotten that there was a small thermal area at Koutu, 1.6 km north of Ohinemutu. The principal spring formed a large pool, Tapui Te Koutu, 18 to 24 m deep. With westerly or southerly winds the pool was 32 to 38°C, but if the wind changed to north or east the water rose 1.2 m and the temperature increased to 82°C. It was not a pool to leap into in the dark. It is interesting to

Wonders of the Hot Lake District.

——o——

GEYSER HOTEL,

WHAKAREWAREWA

Two miles from Rotorua.

———— •●• ————

THIS place offers advantages to the Tourist and Invalid which cannot be found elsewhere. Here everything is as nature made it, and is totally free from the semi-state of civilization which exists in the township of Ohinemutu.

The GEYSER HOTEL is especially adapted for invalids, being quite close to the celebrated "Spout" and "Oil" Baths.

THE "SPOUT" or "TURIKORE" BATH.

This bath has been pronounced by members of the medical profession, who have had an opportunity of testing it, as the best spring in the Rotorua District for the cure of CHRONIC RHEUMATISM in almost all its forms. It is here one has the advantage of the Hot Douche, the value of which to invalids is so well known. The following, amongst other diseases, are certain of cure by this bath :—

RHEUMATISM—Chronic, Muscular and Articular
LUMBAR NEURALGIA—LUMBAGO SCIATICA—KIDNEY AND LIVER
  COMPLAINTS—CERTAIN DISEASES OF THE SKIN, such as
  PSORIASIS, ECZEMA, etc., etc.

THE "OIL" BATH.

This bath is famous for its cure of Cutaneous Diseases. It is distinctly sedative, if not soporific in its action.

THE "ALUM" BATH.

This spring is noted for its efficacy in the treatment of certain cases of abdominal congestion. Cases of severe hœmorrhoids have been cured by this water.

"ARIKIKAPAKAPA" or "JACK'S BATH."

This bath is the furthest from the hotel, being about a quarter of a mile distant. It has been lately renovated, and is now suitable for use. This spring is similar in composition and action to, the Priest's Bath at the Government Sanatorium. It is generally used in conjunction with the Spout Bath if the case requires it.

To the visitor in search of the beautiful and marvellous, to the naturalist thirsting for knowledge, Whakarewarewa and its surroundings can offer the desiderata. It is now admitted that since the Rotomahana Terraces have disappeared, Whakarewarewa is the most interesting and wonderful spot in the Hot Lake District. Here one may spend days and weeks rambling through the "Geyser Valley," viewing its beauties, and examining its wonders without the fear of *ennui*. The Arikikapakapa steam-holes and mud-volcanoes of all sizes and activity, also offer entertainment to the traveller.

Guides, Horses and Buggies provided. Private Suites of Rooms for families. Special attention paid to Invalids. The management under the personal supervision of Mrs. Taylor. Wines, Spirits, and Ales of the best brands only. TERMS MODERATE.

J. TAYLOR, Proprietor.

An 1888 advertisement for the Geyser Hotel. It was owned by L. D. Nathan and Co., who brought guests by coach from the firm's other spa hotel at Okoroire. The advertisement mentions that the Arikikapakapa bath, having been renovated, is suitable for use. *Hayr's Tourist Guide — The Hot Lakes of New Zealand, Auckland Institute and Museum Library.*

Papatangi or the Lobster Pool in the Kuirau area, Rotorua, won its Pakeha name from the reddened skins of European bathers. Several people drowned in it. It has now cooled down and is no longer used for bathing. *Auckland Institute and Museum.*

wonder how it was discovered, in such deep hot water, that "Thick masses of confervoid plants line the bottom of the pool".[23] The words were written by the guide and soldier Gilbert Mair, who lived at Koutu in the 1870s. The ubiquitous Robert Graham lived in the same area in the 1880s, providing "several warm springs and a delightful beach for bathing".[24]

A well-known photograph by Alfred Burton, taken at Ohinemutu during July 1886, and looking north, across Koutu, must have been shot in a northerly or easterly wind. There is a mass of steam from the Tapui pool. In 1884 J. H. Kerry Nicholls gave it the name Tupuhi, and described it as being 27 m long.[25] The pool lost its heat during this century and was filled in. Only a little steam on frosty mornings now indicates its position.

Near Ohinemutu there is a widespread group of pools in an area known as Kuirau. The name was taken from a hot lake where kuias from Ohinemutu used to wash clothes in the soft water. Near the lake was a pool with a considerable reputation. It was known as Papatangi, or the Lobster Pool, its later name deriving from the appearance of Europeans after they had bathed in it. The lack of a dressing shed at the Lobster Pool resulted in some correspondence in the Tourist Department file in 1906. A Mr J. T. McIntosh claimed that on several "occasions when in the company of ladies he has frequently seen from 20 to 30 men . . . in various stages of undress".[26]

Women bathed in a small spring known as the Soda Pool. As it was deep, a ladder was placed over it from which bathers suspended themselves. This pool disappeared in 1945 when the spring was used to supply a footpool, which

Waikimihia (Hinemoa's Pool) on Mokoia. This photograph was taken in July 1886. Mud from the Tarawera eruption on 10 June that year partially blocked the outlet and Lake Rotorua rose. Lake water entered the pool until a cut was made in the Ohau Channel. *Photograph by Burton Bros, Rotorua Museum.*

survives as the most easterly of 2 footpools in the reserve. The first, known as the Radium Bath, was developed in 1940 but no longer exists. Around 1905 the idea of using the Kuirau lake as a hot water reservoir for the Rotorua Bathhouse was considered, but the temperature of the lake varied too much.

Legend has made Waikimihia, or Hinemoa's Pool on Mokoia Island in Lake Rotorua, the most famous geothermal bath in the country, but it is only the largest of several baths on the south-eastern side of the island. Apart from the story of Hinemoa and Tutanekai, which took place several hundred years ago, the pool is also notable as being the first mentioned in English literature relating to the Plateau; the Rev. Henry Williams visited and described Mokoia in October 1831.

In August 1849 a house was built at the Manupirua Spring on the south shore of Rotoiti for Thomas Henry Smith who acted as Government Agent in the Rotorua district. One of the people who most enjoyed the pleasures of this cove under a cliff was Thorpe Talbot, who wrote in 1882, "Tattooing our bodies with daubs of soft yellow mud of the spring . . . the night is to be remembered as one of thorough relaxation and enjoyment."[27] This description is all the more fascinating when one remembers that Thorpe Talbot was in fact Mrs Charles Dudley Robert Ward. It was no doubt easier for her to express such sensuality in the guise of a man.

Probably the most sulphurous waters ever used for bathing were the Taheke Hot Springs on the north side of Rotoiti. Some idea of the degree of acidity is given by the following comparisons: the Priest Spring at the Polynesian Pools

Manupirua Bath, Rotoiti, c. 1890. *Photograph by Josiah Martin, Rotorua Museum.*

had, in a 1907 analysis, 3.7 grains of free sulphuric acid per 4.54 l; the New Priest Spring, which formerly supplied the Rotorua Bathhouse and which now is used in the Queen Elizabeth Hospital, had 16.8; the Postmaster Bath had 22.2; the Taheke Sulphur Bath had 152. Fraser's Hot Springs Hotel had a brief history beside these now forgotten springs.

East from Rotorua are the Waitangi Springs at Rotoehu. One of the most lugubrious passages in Volcanic Plateau literature came from the pen of Thorpe Talbot after her visit to Waitangi:

> hundreds of gallons of soda-water, sufficient to cure a whole planet full of dyspeptics . . . Looking on this, and remembering how often the weary soul has longed in vain for sodawater and a red herring early, very early in the morning after a lamp-post has taken the weary body home from 'a little sociable' at a friend's house overnight, we felt that we could weep with yearning for a lodging in the Rotoehu wilderness in whose 'contiguity of shade' one could repose while quarts of effervescing nectar from Nature's own breast were cooled off for one's consumption, and never have to seek wildly through the empty pockets of one's varied vestments for the wherewithal to pay.[28]

The spring Mrs Ward referred to is extremely effervescent and lies to the east of the main bathing area, which is principally supplied by a chalybeate spring.

Bathing at Orakei Korako as seen by the Rev. Richard Taylor in *Te Ika a Maui*, 1855. *Alexander Turnbull Library.*

Above this was, until a few years ago, a hole that emitted poisonous gases. It was full of the bones of birds that had succumbed while flying over it. A forbidding carving used to stand beside it, as a warning. Mrs Ward imagined a future advertisement for Rotoehu Ferrum Sodaline — "Have you a headache? Have you a heartache? Have you a mother-in-law? Do you suffer from neuralgia . . . liver complaint, lunacy, limp shirts, black jack or blind staggers?"[29]

Another minor hot springs area was affected by wind or atmospheric change in the same manner as the large pool at Koutu. Two very hot springs, known as Moku-Tuhana, supply a bath in the Whangapoua Valley area near Atiamuri. Also near Atiamuri, but now under the new Lake Ohakuri, was a pool, Niho-o-te-Kiore, much visited by travellers in the second half of the nineteenth century. Most accounts relate to the early 1870s when Captain Gilbert Mair held a defensive site with Arawa warriors, who were serving as Armed Constabulary. Politician and artist Sir William Fox described the pool in 1874: "on the eastern side of the river, and at its very margin, is a moderate-sized cistern of hot water, capable of containing fifteen or twenty bathers, close packed."[30] Fox suggested that a moderate-sized bathing establishment could be established there.

167

Fox also visited Orakei Korako, where he found a perfect natural "Sitz" bath with elbow rests and polished silica seat, "let in, as it were, into the shallower and wider cistern which surrounds it". The bath contained a considerable suspension of silica which coated the skin of the bather. Fox gave this ngawha a high recommendation: "It was a sensation of Paradise to sit in this bath after a long and hot day's travel, watching the full moon rising above the craggy ridge . . ."[31] It is a pity that the pool is now on the bed of a deep lake. Terence Gordon also expressed his admiration of this pool in *Hot Lakes, Volcanoes and Geysers of New Zealand*, published in 1888: "It is probably the most luxurious and enervating bath of the whole district."[32] Gordon claimed that the name of the ngawha was Mimi-a-homaiterangi — a stream given to the heavens. Waiwhakaata, the pool in the Alum Cave at Orakei Korako, was used for bathing. There was a stone couch at the bottom of the cave on which the Ngati Tahu lay rheumatic people to receive relief from the heat.[33]

Few places in the world have such delightful resources for natural geothermal bathing as Waiotapu. There are 6 hot waterfalls of various heights for spout baths, although probably no more than 100 people have seen the highest of these falls. There are 3 places where hot streams of a considerable volume join the cold Waiotapu Stream. In any such bathing it is vital to heed the Department of Health's warning not to put your head under the water. Amoebic meningitis can be contacted in such situations, usually as a result of jumping or diving into warm water with earth contact. The water has to be forced up the nose for the pathogenic amoeba to reach the area where the olfactory nerves pierce the skull. For absolute safety, the head must be kept out of the water.

Before 1931 there were dressing sheds at the Venus Bath and the Spout Bath. It is unfortunate that the forest had to be felled in 1979 at Kerosene Creek, one of the most unusual bathing areas in the country. In 20 years' time, however, it will look as attractive as it did during the 1960s and 1970s.

Immediately south of Waiotapu there is a private bath in a group of geothermal pools at Opaheke or Otakitaki. At Reporoa, Second World War conscientious objectors from Whenuaroa Camp, Strathmore (in the Broadlands area) built dressing sheds at Butcher's Pool. Where the country's second geothermal power scheme is being developed at Ohaki there was, until the Waikato rose with the filling of the hydro Lake Ohakuri in 1961, a sulphur cave much used by the Ngati Tahu and Ngati Whaoa people of the district for treating rheumatism.

In the Golden Springs area, originally known as Orangikereru, the 2 springs which supply the warm water to the tourist complex are on a farm across the road. Golden carp seem to thrive in the stream, which appears to be chalybeate (containing iron).

Much better known to late nineteenth-century travellers than the Waiotapu or Reporoa pools was the Otamakokore Stream. For a brief period, from 1870 to 1873, the principal route for travellers south of Rotorua was via the gully of Earthquake Road to the Waikite Valley and thence southward along the base of the Te Kopia scarp and followed a small stream valley towards the Waikato, a little below Orakei Korako. In the Waikite Valley they camped beside and bathed in the hot Otamakokore Stream. The valley of this stream was known to the Ngati Whaoa people as Paparata, which meant, literally, "earth doctor" — earth used to cure ailments. People used to bathe at the junction of the Otamakokore with the cold Waro Stream from the Te Kopia Valley. (The latter begins as a warm stream, being the run-off of a thermal area 14 km south of Waikite.)

In 1973 the farmers of the Waikite Valley developed the Otamakokore into a very attractive area of public and private pools. The complex fits neatly into the dramatic landscape of gigantic rocks and scarps leading up to the Opouri or Ngapouri saddle. Eating strudel above the new baths, it is easy to imagine that you are at a small German spa; there is no opera house but the natural scenery is remarkable. Waikite Springs and De Bretts at Taupo are the most attractive of the new geothermal water complexes. Twentieth-century technology is more sensitively implanted upon natural resources than in some hot pool developments of the last 20 years.

In 1908 the Ohine-Ariki hot springs near Mokai, 48 km north-west of Taupo, were recommended as a possible area for curative purposes, but were then considered too remote from Taupo and Rotorua for any development. Exploratory drilling is being carried out at present as this is a major Volcanic Plateau geothermal field and a possible site for a power station to follow Ohaaki at Broadlands. Most of the thermal activity near this former milling settlement is in the form of large mudpools, although at least 1 water pool was much used by the employees of the Taupo Totara Timber Company. The pools belong to the Ngati Te Kohera people, centred around Pukaketaiari House.

The Ketetahi Springs, 1456 m above sea level on 1 side of Tongariro, were used for centuries by the Tuwharetoa people to cure various ailments. In 1901 James Cowan described the situation in *Lake Taupo and the Volcanoes*: "Dense clouds of sulphurous steam envelop us as we clamber up the rock-strewn water-worn gully, at the bottom of which flows an uninviting black stream."[34] It was a little like taking a cure in hell.

The Tarawera Spring is 1 km from a small settlement on the Napier-Taupo Road. After being a bathing area for the local Ngati Hineuru people for several hundred years it became a place of interest for the residents of Napier from 1870 and particularly so 2 years later when a regular coach service to Taupo began. J. Ernest Tinne described Tarawera in that year: "There is a snug little inn for visitors, and a hot spring, to which one ought to be acclimatised, for I came out of the rough wooden tub on the hillside as red as a lobster, and with a disagreeable tightness about the forehead."[35]

When the Tourist Department was created Sir William Russell of Flaxmere and Sherenden estates in Hawke's Bay, helped to persuade the superintendent of the new department to make the spring accessible.[36] The hotel was on a different site to the present tavern — more like 4 km from the spring — and the track was narrow, steep and precarious, as the spring is on a steep slope above the Waipunga River.

Arthur Warbrick, the Rotorua guide, oversaw the construction in 1907. A site was blasted out of the rock cliff and a narrow bathhouse perched over the river,

This photograph of the Tarawera Hot Springs shows the bathhouse perched on the cliff above the Waipunga Stream, about 2 km from the Napier-Taupo Road. A track had to be blasted to the springs. The remnants of the 1870 bathtub can be seen, carried by a slip, towards the stream. *Auckland Weekly, 1907.*

but the distance from the hotel became less of a problem when, shortly before the opening of the bathhouse, the hotel burned down and its replacement was resited. A large party of guests from Napier and the department celebrated the opening in October 1907.

It was the only celebration of any size to take place at the Tarawera Baths. Since 1909 its history has been one of slips, corrosion and abandonment. In 1935 an enormous boulder went through the roof and the bathhouse was locked up at the end of the year. The Lands and Survey Department took over control of the spring in 1962 and in 1963 it was leased to the proprietor of the hotel and, since the second hotel burned down in the 1960s, the owner of the tavern. At present, 2 tubs, open to the sky, provide facilities fairly similar to those Mr Tinne experienced in 1872.

Most of these other springs on the Plateau are still used by local people but they are no longer part of tourist literature, and no invalids visit them.

References

1   Fox, the Hon. W. "Hot Springs District of the North Island" (letter to the Hon. the Premier). *Appendices to the Journal of the House of Representatives*, 1874, H-26.

2   Cowan, James. *The Maoris of New Zealand*, Whitcombe & Tombs, 1910.

3   *Ibid.*

4   *Ibid.*

5   Willis, A. D. *Geysers and Gazers, or, a trip through the boiling springs districts of New Zealand, the wonderland of the world*, Wanganui, Willis, 1888.

6   Bunbury, Clement. "A Visit to New Zealand Geysers" in *Fraser's Magazine*, 1879.

7   Johnson, J. *Notes from a journal kept during an excursion to the boiling springs of Rotorua and Rotomahana . . . in the summer of 1846–1847.*

8   Tinne, J. Ernest. *The Wonderland of the Antipodes; and other sketches of travel in the North Island of New Zealand*, London, Sampson Low, 1873.

9   Trollope, Anthony. *Australia and New Zealand*, Melbourne, Robertson, 1873.

10 *Ibid.*

11 Fox, the Hon. W. *op. cit.*

12 Talbot, Thorpe [pseudonym for Mrs Charles Dudley Robert Ward]. *The New Guide to the Lakes and Hot Springs, and a month in hot water*, Wilson & Horton, 1882.

13 Froude, James Anthony. *Oceana or England and her colonies*, London, Longmans, 1885.

14 *Ibid.*

15 Domett, Alfred. *Ranolf and Amohia*, London, Smith, Elder, 1972.

16 Johnson, J. *op. cit.*

17 Chapman, Thomas. Letters and journals to Church Missionary Society, London, 1830–1869.

18 Lewis, T. Hope. *Medical Guide to the Mineral Waters of Rotorua*, Brett, 1885.

19 *New Zealand Tours and Excursions, Rotorua Tour*, Government Printer, 1898.

20 Lewis, T. Hope. *op. cit.*

21 Harris, J. Chantrey. *The Southern Guide to the Hot Lake District of the North Island of New Zealand*, Dunedin, Daily Times, 1878.

22 *Hot Lakes Chronicle*, 26 July 1902, reprinted in *Rotorua Daily Post*, 9 June 1934.

23 Analysis of mineral waters of New Zealand (papers relating to). *Appendices to the Journal of the House of Representatives*, 1879, H-13.

24 Graham, R. Jnr. *Graham's Guide to the Hot Lakes of New Zealand, Pink and White Terraces, Wairakei Geysers, Huka Falls and Waiwera Hot Springs*, Auckland, Wilson & Horton, 1884.

25 Kerry-Nicholls, J. H. *The King Country; or explorations in New Zealand*, London, Sampson Low, 1884.

26 Memo, 27 November 1906, in Tourist Department file 1904/18.

27 Talbot, Thorpe. *op. cit.*

28 *Ibid.*

29 *Ibid.*

30 Fox, the Hon. W. *op. cit.*

31 *Ibid.*

32 Gordon, Terence. *Hot Lakes, Volcanoes and Geysers of New Zealand, with legends*, Napier, Gordon, 1888.

33 Russell, Arthur. *A Trip Through Taupo and the Hot Lakes*, 1868.

34 Cowan, James. *Lake Taupo and the Volcanoes. Scenes from lake and mountain, and tales from Maori folk-lore*, Auckland, The Observer, 1901.

35 Tinne, J. Ernest. *op. cit.*

36 Sir William Russell, Flaxmere, Hastings, to the Colonial Secretary, 17 October 1902.

24 More Springs off the Plateau

Most geothermal springs outside the Volcanic Plateau are in the northern half of the North Island. Apart from Hanmer and Maruia Springs, those of the South Island are small, in remote areas and on the western side of the island. An extreme case of a group of springs known only to trampers and mountaineers is that at Welcome Flat, half a day's climb up the Southern Alps from Westland, on the Copland Track. The effort of reaching the flat is rewarded by an outdoor bath in clear hot water, surrounded by towering peaks. In Europe a spa would have been built in such a setting, but development at Welcome Flat consists of a track created by the Government in 1911 and a hut originally constructed in 1918. Many people would prefer to see the whole area — and the springs — left in an almost natural state.

The north, too, has its remote springs. On Great Barrier Island, for instance, in 2 areas of the Kaitoke River valley, are some of the least known springs in the country. As was the case with most hot springs, the Maori people living there had been using the waters for the treatment of rheumatism and skin complaints long before the first European description. In this instance the author was C. P. Winkelmann, who recorded his visit in 1886.[1] (Winkelmann was the brother of the important photographer, Henry Winkelmann.) There are a large number of springs in and around the headwaters of the stream. Even when Winkelmann visited, he found that Europeans had camped at 2 simple baths to treat rheumatism. He remarked on an oppression of the chest he experienced as a result of gas coming from the springs, and described the strange appearance of the valley at evening and early morning, with clouds of steam. Even today Kaitoke Springs are known only to those living on Great Barrier and to a few trampers.

On the dip slope of the Kaimai Range, and not very far, in a direct line, from Te Aroha, are the Sapphire Springs near Katikati. Their discovery (at least their discovery by Europeans) is recounted in Arthur Gray's *An Ulster Plantation* of 1938. Six boys went hunting for shags' nests in the Christmas holidays of 1879. "In the bush they found a ditch with hot water and steam rising, so they stripped off and took turns to lie down in it. Their parents told them their story was a fairy tale, but they went back many times afterwards."[2] The springs were developed into baths, in 1897, by the owner of the Junction Hotel, which stood where the Te Aroha track met the Tauranga-Waihi Road. By 1900 there were 3 baths and in 1906 the Government considered acquiring the springs. The Balneologist thought that the fairly neutral water could be bottled as an excellent table water.

Welcome Flat Hot Springs, Copland Pass. It is probably the most remote hot spring in the country, and also probably the only one without a long history of Maori use before European exploration. There would have been little reason for the Ngati Mamoe or Kai Tahu people of the southern South Island to cross the Southern Alps in this area. *Alexander Turnbull Library.*

Kaitoke Hot Springs, Great Barrier Island. Henry Winkelmann took the only well-known photographs of the area and his brother, C. P. Winkelmann, provided the best description of the springs. *Auckland Institute and Museum.*

Sapphire Springs was developed as a holiday place in the late 1920s. The geothermal water is now obtained by bore, which is the only trace of the natural pool.

On the opposite coast, the Kawhia Chamber of Commerce in 1919 considered the Government should develop the springs found below high water mark, 1.6 km north of the settlement. Known as the Te Puia Springs, they have a similar situation to those at Hot Water Beach on the east coast of the Coromandel Peninsula. The Tourist Department was sufficiently interested to try and arrange side trips from Waitomo to the Kawhia springs in 1946.

Of much more significance and extent are the hot springs at Miranda in the Hauraki Gulf. Early this century there were something like 100 springs over a 40 ha area. Thirty of them now supply a 250,000 gallon pool. The original name for this area is Pukorokoro and the springs were used by the Ngati Paoa people. The European name came from a British gunboat in action on the Firth of Thames in 1863. Because of the lack of road access until well into this century, this group of springs remained undeveloped much longer than many smaller spring localities. One of the first European owners was J. Pond, who carried out many of

Wai-te-Puia Springs, Maketu, c. 1910. *Whakatane Museum.*

the early analyses of spring water throughout the country. He must have been disappointed that the Government twice refused, in 1903 and 1913, to purchase the Miranda Springs.

A 1910 photograph showed the largest natural pool set in a peat swamp. Most development was carried out after the Second World War and today's complex and resort includes private pools, children's pools and the largest geothermal bath in the country.

The Onepu Springs, across the Tarawera River from Kawerau, have partly disappeared. The by-products of industry have covered some of the springs at Rotoitipaku, a small lake that is the centre of the field. Sulphur was being extracted from this thermal area as early as 1886 and the geothermal field, which provides power for the Tasman Pulp and Paper Company, is very much larger than that of the nearby Awakeri Springs. Because the latter area was developed for recreational purposes it is better known than Onepu Springs.

The springs are owned by Ngati Umutahi of the Tuwharetoa people, and until 1950, when developmental work began at Kawerau, members of the Savage family used to ferry visitors across the Tarawera River to the natural baths. The area is mentioned in the 1898 *New Zealand Tours and Excursions*: "Passing the little lakes Rotorua and Rotoitipaku, the road [the old Whakatane–Rotorua coach road] descends to the Tarawera River flat; where a track leads off to the right to Te Onepu, with its sulphur beds and several good hot baths."[3] In 1921 the Balneologist recommended that the Government purchase the springs. As late as the 1940s, Bradbury's guide to the Bay of Plenty advised people to drive the 8 km down from the new road and be carried by punt across to the springs.

Langbridge and Edgecumbe's guide of 1875 recommended the "Waitepura"[4] Hot Springs near Maketu; the correct name is Waitepuia. In 1909 the Government considered the possibility of leasing and purchasing the springs and developing them. A concrete bath was built in 1923 and the Government again looked at ways "to secure the springs"[5] but they remained in private hands. During the 1970s the baths were run as a commercial venture.

Paeroa's spring of mineral water was investigated by the Government Balneologist in 1904. Because it was not highly mineralised it was suitable for bottling as a table water rather than a medicinal mineral water. There was, however, some iron in the Paeroa water and the Balneologist noted that, as a result, it blackened whisky. Apart from its use with spirits, he remarked of its general potential: "I am afraid however that the universal use of tea in the Colony makes the demand for such a water very limited."[6]

The spring had been commercialised in the 1890s by the Paeroa Water Company, but it was only after 1907, with the second owner, Menzies and Company, that the water became famous. The addition of lemon juice or extract created the popular drink, Lemon and Paeroa, and the industry is symbolised by the giant "L and P" bottle near the centre of the town.

In the days of Hatrick's fleet of river steamers on the Wanganui, the firm invited the Balneologist in 1906 to investigate a hot spring near Pipiriki. Because of the presence of iodine, he recommended it as a medicinal drinking water. At the end of 1907 a track was formed to the spring, and a small summerhouse constructed over a drinking fountain. Men's and women's bathhouses were built. In 1907 Hatrick and Company advertised the Pipiriki Thermal Spring Baths, but thereafter Hatrick's miniature spa disappeared from tourist literature, and although the spring still exists there is nothing left of the bath.

Several groups of hot springs could compete for the title of the most inaccessible in the country, and Puketitiri is a definite contender. When the locals petitioned the Government in 1909 to open up the springs to the public, they claimed that there was a good metalled road from Napier to Puketitiri, a distance of 56 km, and a formed but unmetalled road for 9.6 km. (Having experienced the longer section in the 1940s and 1950s, I doubt whether most visitors would have enjoyed the unmetalled portion.) Beyond that there was a considerable walk. The petitioners recommended that the road be continued up the Mohaka River to link with the Napier-Taupo Road. (At Te Haroto, travellers are not very far, by direct line, from the Puketitiri Springs, but there is no road connection.)

It was 11 km from the end of the unmetalled road to the springs, with a 1 m path over this stretch and then a narrow zigzag track down the cliff to the place

PIPIRIKI
Thermal Spring
BATHS.

Towels and Keys for Bath Rooms can be obtained from the Manager, Pipiriki House.

ANALYSIS OF WATER.

Sodium Chloride	... ...	121·88
Potassium Chloride	... ... Traces	·52
Magnesium Iodide	... ... Traces	
Calcium Sulphate	... ...	1·88
Aluminium Chloride	... ...	1·22
Sodium Carbonate	... ...	·48
Magnesium Carbonate	... ...	2·22
Silica	... ...	2·41
	Total Solids	180·61

Dr. Wohlmann, Govt. Balneologist, states:

" Taken in regular doses, and on an empty stomach, it would act as a very gentle tonic in certain forms of Dyspepsia, by cleansing the stomach, and stimulating the gastric and intestinal mucous membranes. For internal administration the water is specially adapted. For this purpose it should be taken fresh at the spring before the three principal meals, the walk back to Pipiriki afterwards being rather an advantage, except in debilitated subjects. Aerated it should make an excellent table water.

The small amount of Silica present is an especial advantage in a country where most of the mineral springs are too Siliceous. The water would be classed as ' muriated ' the chief constituent being Sodium Chloride ; but the small quantity of Magnesium Iodide present is of much more importance than would be indicated by the analysis, as this Iodide tends to decomposition at the source, with the consequent liberation of free Iodide. Iodide in this ' nascent ' condition has more powerful properties than in its ordinary state."

THERE IS A DRINKING FOUNTAIN AT THE SPRING

Also Bathrooms for Ladies and Gentlemen.

A. HATRICK & Co.,
Proprietors Wanganui River Steamer Fleet.

Like Waiho and Haupiri on the West Coast of the South Island, this 1907 bathhouse on a bend of the upper Wanganui River has been forgotten. *National Archives.*

where visitors bathed. The main spring is 45 m above the Mohaka River, on a cliff overlooking the river. Bathers simply stood in the waterfall. The nearest accommodation house was 20 km away at Puketitiri. In 1912 there were plans to erect a simple bathhouse and bunkhouse at this spring but the scheme was turned down because of the difficulty of getting materials to the site. At that stage there was a gap of only 4 km between the metalled road and the springs. Trampers still enjoy the hot waterfall and springs further up the valley, including a fibreglass bath in the middle of the bush.

Over a kilometre south-east of Puriri, at the foot of the Coromandel Range, is a spring of soda water which was formerly of some importance. As early as 1870 the water was shipped to Auckland in kegs and bottled. Campbell and Ehrenfried's Puriri water was on the market until the 1960s. Several places around the Tauranga Harbour obtain hot water by bore — Welcome Bay, Mount Maunganui, Plummer's Point, Omokoroa — and at the Fernland Spa a table water is bottled. None of the Tauranga Harbour baths (apart from the Sapphire Springs) had natural geothermal pools before the drilling which took place in the 1970s.

As socially important as the springs at Miranda are the Waingaro Hot Springs in the Waikato, 26 km from Ngaruawahia, which have become very popular with Hamilton people. Because produce from the Waikato was shipped out through Raglan, the Waingaro Hotel is an historic halfway house. The first primitive bath was constructed at the same time as the hotel, in 1885, and replaced by a concrete bath in 1895. A visit by the Governor-General's party in 1902 brought Waingaro some publicity. According to a *Herald* report, "The party, and particularly the Countess of Ranfurly, were delighted with the Waingaro Hot Springs, and no wonder, for the bath, edged by the beautiful stream, and half shut in by a great wall of forest trees and giant ferns, is a most charming bathing place."[7] The bathhouses were washed out by a flood in 1907 and again in the 1950s. After the second flood the spring water was pumped to an open swimming bath. An attractive new complex of pools and chutes has been developed during the 1970s and 1980s. The extensive development has been made possible by the high yield of the Waingaro Springs — 19,430 l per hour.

A hot spring on Motuhora (Whale Island) was analysed in 1878 but was unsuitable for bathing as the water contained 138 grains of free sulphuric acid per 4.54 l. Although the waters on White Island contain an enormous amount of hydrochloric acid, which would destroy any body immersed in them, proposals were made even for these springs. Spencer's guide suggested in 1885: "White Island is sure some day to become a celebrated sanatorium. Rheumatism, throat and chest affections are frequently cured by a mere residence on the island for a short time."[8]

Spencer's interest in White Island resulted from the small ship *Staffa* making trips for cargoes of sulphur and gypsum. The raw materials were processed at J. A. Wilson's New Zealand Manure and Chemical Company's works at the tip of the Tauranga peninsula. Certainly, with strange cures in fashion in the Northern Hemisphere in the second half of the nineteenth century, it was not beyond belief that patients could be landed on a volcano to breathe fumes. North of Waingaro 2

After Te Aroha water, the table water from Puriri, between Thames and Paeroa, was next in popularity from 1890 to 1930, although it was rivalled by mineral waters from Kamo, Paeroa and Wairongoa (near Dunedin). Advertisement in the *Auckland Weekly*, Christmas Number, 1903. *D. Stafford, Rotorua.*

Waingaro in about 1950. The hotel is very old. It was once the halfway house for the export of wool from the Waikato, through Raglan. The bath in the foreground was constructed in the 1930s for cold water but had the hot water piped into it in 1957. The hot springs are now under separate management. *Pilling family, Waingaro Thermal Baths.*

large springs which have been known variously as the Whangape, the Awaroa, the Naike, the Waiora, and Te Maire Springs. R. Gillies journeyed up the Awaroa Stream, by canoe and on foot, into the forest around the springs in 1868, and the account of his visit was published the following year. The difficulty Gillies had in getting to the spring indicated the lengths to which nineteenth-century travellers would go to see thermal activity. These springs were offered for sale to the Government in 1908, but at that stage, with the cost of the Rotorua Bathhouse, spas were becoming a less attractive proposition.

Camille Malfroy was sent from Rotorua in 1893 to examine some insignificant springs at Hende's Ferry on the Wanganui River in South Westland. His report told of the pathetic occurrence of people being stranded on the far side of the river when, on stormy nights, the ferryman could not hear their cries. As Malfroy's report became a Parliamentary paper, a bell was rapidly installed. After the turn of the century it must have seemed as though the Government had become obsessional about spas and hot springs. The 2 extreme instances of baths or bathhouses in unlikely areas were at Waiho and Haupiri on the West Coast. The 1905 report for the Department of Tourist and Health Resorts mentioned that a small bathhouse had been erected at the junction of the Callery and Waiho Rivers. This was in the forest, some distance from the settlement at Franz Josef Glacier, and has since been affected by a flood.

In 1885, when this photograph of White Island was taken, Spencer's guide suggested that the island would one day become a sanatorium, claiming that merely living there was sufficient to cure many ailments. The guide did not warn that invalids would have to be careful not to be overcome by hydrochloric acid fumes. *Photograph by Charles Spencer, Rotorua Museum.*

Even more remote was the bath and accommodation hut at Haupiri, which is 96 km from Reefton, 64 km from Greymouth and inland from Lake Brunner. To get to the Haupiri or Kopara Hot Springs in 1902 you had to follow a pack track, 1.2 m wide, through thick bush, from the small (and now non-existent) settlement of Hatters to the head of Lake Haupiri. Beyond that, Frank Moorhouse, inspecting the site for the Tourist Department, rode some distance along a riverbed to an isolated house. From there a 1.8 m track had been cut to the Haupiri River, and then there were 8 km of rough riverbed. Despite this difficult access, the department built a 2-roomed cottage and a concrete bath at the main spring in 1906. Without a caretaker the bath tended to fill up with leaves and other debris.

In the 1920s the department still had some enthusiasm for the area — "These springs are certainly capable of further development and must inevitably become a potential minor resort."[9] — but it has since been almost forgotten. The last recorded report, in 1945, stated: "the bath is not in good order and is very rough and the inflow of water so small it takes considerable time to get sufficient for a bath."[10]

Haupiri and Waiho represented the ultimate in the Tourist Department's efforts to provide geothermal bathing facilities throughout the country. It is no wonder that the department was besieged with requests from land agents for the

181

inspection of odd hot puddles. Places like Waiho and Haupiri are less well known today than they were 50 years ago. In an age when aches and pains can be easily relieved by medication, there is not the incentive to tramp for long distances through difficult country to find healing hot water.

References

1   Winkelmann, C. P. "Notes on the hot springs nos. 1 and 2, Great Barrier Island" in *Transactions of the New Zealand Institute*, Vol. XIX, 1886.

2   Gray, Arthur J. *An Ulster Plantation: the story of the Katikati settlement*, Wellington, A. H. & A. W. Reed, 1938.

3   *New Zealand Tours and Excursions, Rotorua Tour*, Government Printer, 1898.

4   Langbridge and Edgecumbe. *The Handbook to the Bay of Plenty and Guide to the Hot Lakes . . .,* Tauranga, Langbridge & Edgecumbe, 1875.

5   J. B. Thompson, Under Secretary of Lands and Survey, to the General Manager, Department of Tourist and Health Resorts, 15 November 1923. Tourist Department file 7/27.

6   A. S. Wohlmann to Superintendent, Department of Tourist and Health Resorts, 24 January 1905. Tourist Department file 1902/18.

7   *New Zealand Herald*, 1902.

8   *Spencer's Illustrated Guide to the Hot Springs of Rotorua and Taupo and Other Places of Interest in the Lake District . . .,* Auckland, Murray & Spencer, 1885.

9   E. Dollimore, Tourist Department agent at Greymouth, to General Manager, Department of Tourist and Health Resorts, 1 November 1927. Tourist Department file 20/123.

10   Nancarrow & Co., land and estate agents, Greymouth, to General Manager, Department of Tourist and Health Resorts, 18 December 1945.

Epilogue

Although today more New Zealanders than ever before bathe in geothermal waters, especially in the large pools of such places as Parakai, Waiwera, Miranda, Waingaro and Taupo, there has been no spa in New Zealand in the last 20 years.

Despite the work of the Queen Elizabeth Hospital and the recreational resources of the Polynesian Pools, James Stewart, the author of a visionary scheme for a great South Pacific spa, would probably be disappointed in the Rotorua of the 1980s.[1] Te Aroha has the architectural ghost of a spa history; Hanmer scarcely has even that. Almost nothing remains of some Government efforts to create small local spas. At Te Puia, for example, there is only the skeleton of a building, half hidden in trees.

Few people gave the Government town and intended spa of Rotorua much chance of success in the 1880s. At that time, largely because of easy access via the railway, the rival spa of Te Aroha seemed to offer much greater promise. (The railway did not reach Rotorua until 1894.) Rotorua also suffered because it offered only plain accommodation and little in the way of entertainment.

In those years 3 classes of visitors journeyed to Rotorua, Te Aroha and Hanmer: the large majority were general tourists, some were genuinely sick and desperately seeking a cure, a few came for the fashionable equivalent of a European spa holiday. This small group, important because of its wealth and prestige, was not really catered for until close to the First World War.

The Rotorua Bathhouse provided some of the facilities such visitors sought but also, in the long run, became the principal cause of the abandonment of the spa philosophy in New Zealand. The large amount of money invested in Rotorua meant that it became a yardstick for the success or failure of New Zealand spas. Had Rotorua been a financial success, it would have continued to develop more on European lines, and it is possible that Te Aroha at least would have followed suit.

The course of Government development of and then disengagement from hot springs areas forms a parabola. The base line of the curve was the 1880 situation of natural springs and pools. The curve began with small-scale development at Rotorua, Hanmer and Te Aroha, growth continued with the creation of the Department of Tourist and Health Resorts in 1901 and the apex was reached with the opening of a new area of the Rotorua Bathhouse in 1911. Four years of few visitors and poor maintenance during the First World War began the curve's downward track. The failure of the £30,000 (probably equivalent to some $15,000,000 today) Rotorua Bathhouse to attract sufficient business, the building's unique physical problems, the Depression, the Second World War and a change of philosophy caused the spa curve to plummet until the Government withdrew from the spa business in 1966, at Rotorua, and in 1971, throughout the country.

There were other reasons why spas disappeared. During the peak 1902–11 period of Government finance, there was an absurd degree of development in such remote places as Haupiri and Waiho. It could have been more effective for the Government to have concentrated its spending on Rotorua, Te Aroha and Hanmer, rather than spreading the available money over Morere, Te Puia, Parakai, Maruia, Tarawera and Taupo (the second AC Baths). It may, of course, have been difficult to rationalise such a policy to a voting public. As it was, the Government was under pressure to give every hot water spot the same treatment as Rotorua.

On the other hand, the Government did evade pressure to become involved in Ngawha, Kamo, Waiwera, Miranda, Waingaro, Naike, Matamata, Kawhia, Maketu, Katikati, Paeroa, the Spa and the Terrace Baths at Taupo, Wairakei, Awakeri, Onepu and Puketitiri. Some of these places were, for a time, successfully developed by private enterprise, well-sited Waiwera being the outstanding example, but whether some of the smaller Government spa areas would have been similarly successful under private control is open to question. In some places, however, such as Te Puia, Government interest was distinctly reluctant.

During the 1920s and 1930s, the Government's commitment sometimes appeared half-hearted. With the terrible problem of the Rotorua Bathhouse costs, the Government was probably happy to heed the advice of Dr Lennane when, in the 1940s and 1950s, he advocated the abandonment of the European spa philosophy. Although he was representing a medical opinion, in the long run it had very considerable social effects.

Another factor in the decline of the spas was a gradual change in public attitude — a shift in fashion brought about partly by technology. From the 1920s, the motor car took New Zealand families to the beach; rest cures took place at baches, on sand and in surf. The words "invalid" and "sanatorium" almost disappeared from tourist literature after 1920. People came to think of hot pools in terms of recreation rather than "the cure". There were, too, fewer reports of miraculous cures since, by the 1940s, doctors had other treatments for rheumatic and arthritic conditions. Living conditions were better and diet generally had improved. Also, of course, the tourist trade would not be helped by suggesting to foreign visitors that New Zealand's spas were populated by masses of invalids.

A final important reason for the failure of New Zealand spas was the country's geographical position. The extraordinary range of geothermal resources did not compensate for the distance from Europe and there were not enough people in New Zealand to make expensive hot pool developments pay. Although New Zealand's spas were not ultimately a success, they produced some delightful by-products in the form of Edwardian Rotorua, Te Aroha and Hanmer, and some of the flavour of those days still lingers to remind modern New Zealanders of a nineteenth-century dream to create a great spa in the South Seas.

References
1   Stewart, James. *On the Establishment of a Grand Hotel and Sanatorium in the Rotorua District*, Auckland, Wilson & Horton, 1884.

Appendix: Efficacy

Opinion has always been divided as to how effective hot water bathing is as a treatment for various ailments, especially over the last 40 years. As far back as 1847 Dr Johnson, the Colonial Surgeon, expressed his view while commenting on the medical use of geothermal waters at Tikitere: "I should imagine that their uniform heat is the most effective agent in the cure."[1]

This mid-nineteenth-century opinion was much closer to the medical beliefs of 100 years later than was the attitude of spa practitioners of the 1890s. At that time, as is evident from the report William Pember Reeves returned to the New Zealand Premier in 1897,[2] both a medical mystique and a social aura surrounded European spas. It was hinted that only a very few people, notably a Professor Fresenius of Germany, were capable of analysing geothermal or mineral waters for spa purposes. Certainly some of the doctors concerned with New Zealand waters seemed to accept that their efficacy lay largely in the salts and the search developed in the 1870s and 1880s for unique and effective waters. Analysts were particularly asked to search for lithium salts, which were useful in treating gout and kidney stones. Part of the mystique and the reason for the search was the belief that salts found in natural form were more beneficial than synthetic salts. This also explains the analyses of springs 10, 20 and 30 miles from the nearest settlement. If pools could be found which really did cure rheumatism then the country stood to make a great deal of money. The hunt for pools with near miraculous properties paralleled the research of present-day drug companies.

Even in the 1890s, however, one of the men concerned with the future of New Zealand's spas warned that people expected too much from the chemical constituents of geothermal waters. Dr Ginders, Medical Officer at Rotorua, wrote: "Patients . . . are always anxious to see the analysis of the waters in which they bathe, and are usually under the impression that they absorb into their systems the entire list of salts enumerated. This is an error. The body cannot absorb any salts from an aqueous solution."[3]

The third Balneologist, Dr Blair, agreed with that opinion, in 1944: "the effect of mineral baths [depends] largely on the action of heat plus moisture applied locally or generally for a prolonged period: the salts in solution merely adding to the effect and it appears to be of little importance whether these dissolved salts are chlorides, carbonates, or sulphates . . . The major exception to this is the presence of free sulphuric acid, which has a definite effect upon the skin, and the surface circulation, as in the Priest and Postmaster Baths at Rotorua."[4]

Dr Lennane, the Director of Physical Medicine, believed too much had been claimed for the efficacy of waters in the treatment of disease. "Incidentally," he wrote in a 1950 report, "there is no curative property in mineral waters so far as the rheumatic diseases are concerned. Their mineral content cannot penetrate the skin, and the beneficial effects are due to the heat and subsequent massage or other form of Physic Therapy."[5]

Not everyone agreed with Lennane and Blair. At the Inter-Departmental Committee inquiry into the future of the Rotorua Bathhouse, in 1957, Dr S. H. Hay of Rotorua stated:

> There is another section of the medical profession who say that the baths by themselves are of no value, but that it is the extra treatment given at the same time, massage or some electrical treatment, which does the trick. Now that is quite wrong, and there are plenty of people . . . walking about New Zealand today who have come here and have had nothing but baths — no extra treatment at all — and they have come away very much relieved.[6]

Dr Hay had more to say on this subject, at a course in rheumatology, in 1963: "A large number of general practitioners tell their patients they can get the same relief in their own baths as they can from Rotorua Baths. This is nonsense . . . I don't get the same relief in an ordinary bath as I get in the Rotorua Baths. Ordinary doctors just do not appreciate the value of the Rotorua Baths."[7]

It is unfortunate that this discussion was carried on in such subjective terms. Dr Isdale, Senior Physician at Queen Elizabeth Hospital, put the debate into perspective in 1966: "there never has been any satisfactory scientific evidence that hot sulphur springs are of any direct curative value in rheumatism . . . on the other hand, there is no satisfactory scientific evidence that there are no curative properties in the springs."[8]

William Thompson, an enthusiast for spa treatments, wrote in 1982 that while spa doctors had not been "as conscientious as they might have been in producing evidence to support their claims", more important from his point of view was the fact that "those scientific rheumatologists who are condemning spa therapy . . . have not produced a shred of convincing 'scientific' evidence to show that spa therapy is not as effective as, if not better than, the modern methods they vaunt so proudly." He added, "if British rheumatologists are right, then the majority of European doctors are wrong."[9] Dr Lennane was a British rheumatologist.

In contrast to Dr Lennane's statement that the mineral content of spa waters could not penetrate the skin, Japanese research tends to suggest that he was not correct. Working with isotopes, the researchers have proven that some ions can penetrate the skin. Whether there is any therapeutic effect remains to be proven.[10]

Any clinical discussion of geothermal waters must include the discovery in 1965 of primary amoebic meningoencephalitis, usually called amoebic meningitis. This normally fatal condition is caused by pathogenic amoeba penetrating the brain through the olfactory nerve cords. Thus contact is through the nose. The amoeba can be found in any warm or hot pools with earth contact. Even the casings of bores have to be periodically examined to make certain that there is no infiltration of surface waters. Bathers are, however, safe in any pool with earth contact if they do not immerse their heads. Up until 1979 there were 8 recorded cases of this disease in New Zealand.[11] It has had an effect upon the social aspect of geothermal bathing. In many places where baths are used for swimming and diving geothermal water has been replaced by heated town supply water.

References

1   Johnson, Dr J. *Notes from a Journal kept during an Excursion to the Boiling Springs of Rotorua and Rotomahana . . . in the summer of 1846 and 1847.*

2   Reeves, William Pember. "Our Thermal Springs and their development", memorandum for the Premier Richard Seddon, November 1897. Tourist Department files, National Archives.

3   Ginders, Alfred. *The Thermal Springs District and the Government Sanatorium at Rotorua*, Wellington, Government Printer, 1897.

4   Blair, A. J. Report on Ngawha, 1944. Health Department files, National Archives.

5   Dr G. H. Q. Lennane. Report on Queen Elizabeth Hospital 1950. Health Department files, National Archives.

6   Dr S. H. Hay. Testimony to Inter-Departmental Committee, November 1957. Health Department files, National Archives.

7   Dr S. H. Hay. Statement at course in rheumatology at Queen Elizabeth Hospital, 1963. Tourist Department file 20/120.

8   *Daily Post*, 25 July 1966.

9   *Royal Society of Health Journal*, Vol. 102, No. 5, October 1982.

10 Nohara, H. "The penetration of mineral water constituents" in Licht, S. *Medical Hydrology*, New Haven, Licht, 1963.

11 Collins. C. M. *Up to Your Neck in Water*, Department of Health leaflet, 1979.

Index

V. R. WARD, GOVERNMENT PRINTER, NEW ZEALAND — 1986

59610/E — 86PTK